FIELD MUSIC:
From Antietam to Andersonville
The Civil War Letters of Lyman B. Wilcox

Lyman B. Wilcox, ca. 1873

Berlin Historical Society
Berlin, Connecticut

The Berlin Historical Society, Inc.
PO Box 8192
305 Main Street
Kensington, CT 06037
www.berlincthistorical.org

The Berlin Historical Society is a non-profit organization exploring the depths of Berlin, Connecticut's rich history. We offer exhibits throughout the year to showcase the development of Berlin, as well as America as a whole, throughout time. Though our largest annual exhibit takes place at the Berlin Fair, we also offer exhibits and tours within the museum throughout the year. We are also always open to calls and questions from those curious about Berlin's past, as well as those who wish to get involved in uncovering its past.

Library of Congress Control Number: 2012944851
Field Music: From Antietam to Andersonville - The Civil War Letters of Lyman B. Wilcox / Sarah M. Caliandri, Lisa M. Jacobs, Nancy A. Moran

ISBN 978-0-615-67178-9

This book is dedicated to Berlin, Connecticut veterans, past and present, and to those who have loved and supported them. The cost of your service cannot be measured in gold or silver, but you have our eternal gratitude.

TABLE OF CONTENTS

Acknowledgments

The Berlin Historical Society and the authors would like to acknowledge the many people who helped make this book possible. Innumerable thanks are due to Steve Buckley, who first transcribed the Civil War letters and performed the initial research. The donors of the Lyman and Robert Wilcox letters also have our eternal gratitude. We also thank Melody Carter for her general assistance and Bill Caughman for help with research involving the 16th Connecticut Regiment's flags. Our proofreaders Dante Caliandri, Janice Jacobs, and Rick Ladizki also deserve our gratitude. Finally, additional thanks go to all those who research and preserve the history of Berlin, Connecticut and its residents.

Introduction

This book, built around a compilation of letters from the 1850s to 1870s, tells the story of Lyman Bulkley Wilcox (Lyman B.), his family and friends of Berlin, Connecticut, as they lived in times of both personal and national tumult. The bulk of the letters are from 1862-1864, when Lyman B. was a drummer in the 16th Connecticut Volunteers, Co. G. He enlisted in 1862 at the tender age of 17, joining a brand-new regiment that was baptized in the blood of Antietam only three weeks after leaving Connecticut. On April 20, 1864 Lyman B. was captured along with the rest of his regiment at the siege of Plymouth, North Carolina, and was sent to the infamous Andersonville Prison Camp in Georgia. He survived eight months as a prisoner of war in Andersonville and possibly also in Florence, South Carolina.

Lyman B.'s letters give us insight into the day-to-day life lived by a teenage boy and Union soldier one hundred and fifty years ago. Letters written before and after the war form a picture of a family touched by tragedy and hope. Additional research obtained from local records and histories provides insight into the people mentioned in the letters and determines their relationships.

Many of the letters were written to Lyman B.'s younger brother, Robert. The closeness of these two is evident in the tone of the letters, which remains upbeat throughout most of the correspondence. Lyman consistently maintains the attitude of the caring big brother looking out for his little brother and family.

The small New England town of Berlin, Connecticut that Lyman B. knew when he enlisted was quite different than the town of Berlin today. In the mid-nineteenth century, Berlin was mainly an agricultural town, with a number of cottage industries, many of them located along the numerous streams and rivers. The town consisted of two sections: Kensington, the western side of town, and Worthington, the eastern part. New Britain, once a part of Berlin, had recently separated from the town, but ties remained strong between the communities.

Introduction

The tin industry, which had sent the Yankee Peddler all over the eastern seaboard, was beginning to fade, along with the small shops that had supported it. The brick industry which would define the town for the next 100 years was only just beginning. The iconic meeting house in Worthington had recently suffered a fire, and a new church was built to replace it. The thrifty parishioners transferred the building to the town and it had begun its second life as town hall for Worthington. Worthington Ridge, which Lyman called home for several years before his enlistment, was known as Berlin Street, Main Street, or simply, 'the street'.

In Kensington, the attack on Fort Sumter inspired Rev. Elias Hilliard of the Kensington Congregational Church to put down the sermon he had prepared for that day. He instead preached a fiery discourse that stirred the hearts of the faithful. Later in the war, parishioner and noted artist Nelson Augustus Moore designed a brownstone monument to commemorate those who had died in the war. It was dedicated July 28, 1863, and is claimed to be the first Civil War monument in the country.

Civil War monument in Kensington, CT, designed by Nelson Augustus Moore and built in 1863. Photo ca. 1910.

Ladies of the church also labored to construct a flag which flew over the church during the course of the war. It remains in the church's possession.

Lyman B. was a musician. He prepared for his enlistment by learning the basic military tunes that were used in the service. Since the fourteenth century fifes and drums have been used to enhance martial activity, first in Europe and then in America. During the Civil War it regulated marches and practice maneuvers, daily camp activities, and was a vital part of ceremonies, such as parades and funerals. Each infantry company was assigned a drummer and a fifer. A musician could also be assigned to hospital duty when needed. Lyman's position as a musician may have protected him from injury on the battlefield, especially at Antietam. However, it did not protect him from the diseases that ran through the camps like wildfire. The use of field musicians declined after the War because of the advent of more accurate weapons and better means of communication. The music and its traditions live on in the ancient fife and drum corps, modern groups of today who portray and play the music of historical field musicians in reenactments, parades and other events.

The letters in the following chapters were transcribed verbatim, using the spelling and grammar of the writer. Questionable words have been marked with question marks. Clarifications have been placed in italic *[brackets]*. Soldiers' names in **bold** indicate that further information about their service can be found after the letter. Information about most names mentioned in the letters can be found in the Cast of Characters before the first chapter. Limited information on the Sixteenth Connecticut Volunteer Infantry has been included at the beginning of each chapter to provide context for Lyman B.'s letters and experiences.

Cast of Characters in the Letters

Immediate Family

Lyman Bulkley Wilcox – (Jan. 20, 1845 - May 29, 1875) Writer of the letters. He is buried in Maple Cemetery, Berlin.

Robert M. Wilcox – (Jun. 3, 1849 – May 21, 1916) Lyman B.'s younger brother. He lived in Berlin, New Britain, and then Meriden, CT before marrying famed poet Ella Wheeler and moving to Branford, CT. His ashes are interred on his estate in Short Beach, Branford, CT.

Hattie – (May 5, 1851 – Mar. 4, 1907) Harriet Louise Wilcox, Lyman B. and Robert Wilcox's younger sister. She married Leander Bunce of Berlin, and later lived in Kensington on the Chamberlain Highway. She is buried in Maple Cemetery, Berlin.

Lyman Wilcox, Sr. – (ca. 1819 – Mar. 10, 1855) Lyman B.'s father. One of seven children, he made tinners' tools through his life. He is buried in Wilcox Cemetery, East Berlin.

Maria or Mia – (Apr. 27, 1821 – Dec. 1, 1858) Maria Bulkley Wilcox, Lyman B.'s mother. She is buried in Wilcox Cemetery, East Berlin.

Others mentioned in the letters, in alphabetical order by first name, then last name

Aggie – (Dec. 3, 1855 – after 1930) Agnes Bulkley Chambers, daughter of Uncle Francis and Aunt Mary (Bulkley) Chambers and Lyman's cousin.

Allen Galpin – (Oct. 23, 1820 – Aug. 26, 1894) Born in Berlin to Caleb Galpin and Betsy McLean. He married Julia Dickinson in

Berlin and relocated to Springfield, MA before 1850. He was a merchant there, dealing in stoves.

Lt. Andrus - See Wallace Andrews.

Bob Ridley - Possibly a musical tune.

Bryan Atwater – (Jun. 7, 1826 – Jul. 21, 1903) A Berlin resident, he was a well-respected merchant who lived on Worthington Ridge not far from Lyman B.'s Grandmother Bulkley. He is buried in Maple Cemetery, Berlin.

Bryant – (? – Sep. 25, 1864) George Bryant was a fellow musician in the 16th Conn., Co. I. He was from Hartford, CT and enlisted in July, 1862. He was captured at Plymouth, NC on Apr. 20, 1864. He died in a Charleston, SC prison camp Sep. 25, 1864.

Charlie Brandegee – (Dec. 12, 1845 – Sep. 21, 1927) Charles Brandegee was born in Berlin, son of Dr. Elishama Brandegee. He and his family lived just north of Lyman B.'s grandmother on Worthington Ridge.[1] He served in the Civil War, NY 5th Regiment, Co. I, and NY 146th Regiment, Co. A. He and Lyman B. were good friends, and were together as POWs in Andersonville. Later, he lived in Farmington, CT, where he died. His brother, Robert Bolling Brandegee, was a noted artist. Another brother, Townshend, also served in the Civil War. Charles is buried in Maple Cemetery, Berlin.

By Chamberlain, brother Val - Probably Abiram (Dec. 7, 1837 – May 15, 1911) and Valentine (ca. 1833 – Jun. 25, 1893), two brothers who were born in Colebrook, CT, and later moved to New Britain, CT in 1856. Abiram ultimately became a banker and then Governor of Connecticut. He became a resident of Meriden, CT. His brother Valentine became a judge and remained in New Britain. The brothers continued to be close throughout their lives,

---

[1] 1860 U.S. Census

visiting each other every Sunday. The road they used to travel between New Britain and Meriden has been memorialized in the Chamberlain Highway.

Charlie Roys – (ca. 1837 – Jul. 26, 1900) A neighbor from Berlin, he enlisted as a Corporal Aug. 7, 1862 in the 16th Conn., Co. G. He eventually was promoted to Sergeant, was a prisoner at Andersonville, and was mustered out with the regiment in 1865.

Edith – (Apr. 26, 1855 - ?) Edith Booth, daughter of Lester and Harriet (Bulkley) Booth. Younger sister to Hatty and Kittie and cousin of Lyman B.

Edward Parmalee – (ca. 1843 – Sep. 17, 1862) He came from Hartford, CT. Before the war he worked as an apprentice to his father, a dentist. He enlisted in July, 1862 as a Sergeant in the 16th Conn., Co. G, and was killed at the Battle of Antietam.

Uncle Edwin – (ca. 1827 - ?) Edwin Bulkley, Lyman B.'s maternal uncle.

Frank and Wm. Booth – Probably Frank and William H. Booth, two brothers who lived in Bridgeport, CT in 1860. They may have been related to Lyman B.'s Uncle Lester Booth.

Uncle Frank – (May 7, 1828 – Dec. 26, 1912) Francis Chambers, Esq., married Lyman B.'s mother's sister, Mary Adelia Bulkley. He was a lawyer. In 1860 he lived near or on Lower Lane, Berlin. He is buried in Maple Cemetery, Berlin.

Fred Nettleton – (ca. 1846 - ?) He lived with the Washburn family in Berlin in 1860, and would have been a schoolmate of Lyman B. and his brother. He was employed by the New Britain Times and probably reported on the war.

Goodell – (ca. 1846 - ?) Charles Goodell was a drummer from the 16th Conn., Co. B, also referred to as **Charlie G. of Co. B**. He came from Hartford, CT, enlisted in August, 1862, and was mustered out Jun. 24, 1865.

Aunt Hattie and Uncle Lester - Lester Smith Booth (Jan. 19, 1828 – 1898) and Harriet (Bulkley) Booth (ca. 1823 – 1896). Hattie was one of Lyman B.'s mother's sisters, and her husband Lester was a shoemaker. In 1860 and through the time span of Lyman B.'s letters, they lived in New Britain, CT. They are buried in Maple Cemetery, Berlin.

Hatty – (Jul. 14, 1856 - ?) Harriet Bulkley Booth, daughter of Lester and Harriet (Bulkley) Booth. She was Kitty and Edith's sister and also Lyman B.'s first cousin.

Henry Porter – (Jan. 4, 1840 – Jul. 12, 1920) Possibly son of Lotan Porter and Clarissa Beckley (daughter of Elias Beckley and Rachel Savage), making him a distant cousin of Lyman B. He later became a postmaster in Berlin, where he lived on Hudson St. in 1920.

Henry Savage – (ca. 1840 – 1907) Possibly the son of Willis Savage, he was a sergeant in the 16th Conn., Co. G. He was captured Apr. 20, 1864 at Plymouth, NC and imprisoned at Andersonville, GA. He was released in December, 1864. He is buried in Wilcox Cemetery, East Berlin.

Isacc Stanley – Possibly Isaac Stanley of New Britain, who lived near William Buckley, the brother of Lyman B.'s maternal grandfather, Justus Bulkley.

Jim Lamb – (ca. 1845 – 1893) He lived a few houses north of Lyman B.'s grandmother Ruth Bulkley, across from the Berlin Hotel. He was a descendant of James Lamb, inventor of an early cooking stove. He later married and moved to Middletown, CT, where he died. He is buried in Indian Hill Cemetery, Middletown.

Cast of Characters

Jim Whaples – (ca. 1847 – ca. 1916) Son of James B. Whaples, who was hotel keeper of the Berlin Hotel on Worthington Ridge, Berlin.[2] He moved out of town and later lived in New Jersey.[3]

John P. Stannard - A resident of Hartford, CT, he was a principal musician for the 16th Conn. He enlisted in July, 1862, was captured with the rest of the regiment in April, 1864, and was mustered out in June, 1865.

Sgt. Kimball - George R. Kimball lived in Hartford, CT where he worked as a bootcutter as of 1860. He enlisted as a Sergeant Jul. 29, 1862 and was assigned to the 16th Conn., Co. G. He was reduced in rank to Private due to sickness in 1863. He transferred to Co. F Reserve troop in July, 1863 and was discharged in 1865.[4]

Kitty – (Sep. 14, 1854 - ?) Kathryn Booth, daughter of Lester and Harriet (Bulkley) Booth. She was Lyman B.'s first cousin and sister to Hatty and Edith.

Leah - Friend of Robert Wilcox.

Aunt Mary – (Jul. 27, 1830 – Oct. 8, 1877) Mary Bulkley Chambers, wife of Francis Chambers. She was Lyman B.'s maternal aunt. They lived in Berlin while Lyman B. was a child. She and her husband are buried in Maple Cemetery, Berlin.

Capt. Mix – (ca. 1838 – Mar. 8, 1864) Edward H. Mix was the son of James and Lucy Mix and came from a family of locksmiths. He lived in Plymouth, CT in the 1850 and 1860 censuses. He enlisted Jan. 8, 1862 and was commissioned as a Captain. He died on Mar. 8, 1864 in North Carolina.

---

[2] 1860 U. S. Census, also Smith's map of Hartford County, 1855
[3] 1900 U.S. Census
[4] *American Civil War Soldiers* [database on-line]. Provo, UT, USA: Ancestry.com Operations Inc, 1999.

Moses McCrum – (ca. 1832 – Oct. 2, 1864) Born in Ireland and later living in East Berlin, he enlisted as a private in the 16th Conn., Co. G in August, 1862. He was promoted to Corporal in 1863, and promoted again to Sergeant in 1864. He was captured Apr. 20, 1864 at Plymouth, NC, and imprisoned at Andersonville, GA. He died as a POW in Charleston, SC on Oct. 2, 1864. He is buried in Wilcox Cemetery, East Berlin.

Aunt Polly – (Dec. 10, 1797 – Nov. 17, 1865) Polly Savage, sister to Lyman B.'s grandmother Ruth Savage Bulkley. She lived in Berlin.

Riley's store - Possibly a general store in New Britain.

Rob Brandegee – (Apr. 4, 1849 – Mar. 5, 1922) Robert Bolling Brandegee, brother of Charles Brandegee. He became a noted artist and lived in Farmington, CT.

Robbie or Rob – See Robert Wilcox under *Immediate Family*.

Ruth Savage Bulkley – (Jul. 3, 1800 – Nov. 5, 1877) Lyman B.'s maternal grandmother. In 1860 Mrs. Bulkley was living on the east side of Worthington Ridge, Berlin, just north of Hudson Street, with her grandchildren, Lyman, Robert, and Harriet, along with Henry Galpin, merchant, and Mary Coleman, a domestic servant born in Ireland.[5] She is buried in Wilcox Cemetery, East Berlin.

Samuel Ozias Fowler – (Aug. 31, 1822 – Dec. 17, 1906) Cousin of Lyman B., son of Grandma Ruth Bulkley's oldest sister Esther and her husband Ozias Fowler. In the 1850 census he was living with Lyman Wilcox's family on Toll Gate Road and working as a tinner. By 1859, he was a farmer in Branford, CT.

Samuel Woodruff – (Jan. 30, 1843 – Sep. 17, 1863) He lived on Worthington Ridge, Berlin, a little north of the old Meeting House.

---

[5] 1860 U.S. census, Ancestry. com

He enlisted July, 1862 in the 16th Conn. Regiment, Co. G and died in service. He is buried in Maple Cemetery, Berlin.

Taylor – Lyman B.'s New Britain employer in the early 1870s.

Mr. Tibbals of East Berlin – (ca. 1822 – Jul. 31, 1864) Henry Tibbals lived in East Berlin where he made tinners' tools. He was a Corporal in the 16th Conn. Regiment, Co. G. He was captured along with Lyman B. and died in Andersonville, GA of disease. He is buried in Wilcox Cemetery, East Berlin. His son, William Tibbals was also in Co. G and captured with the regiment. He died at Andersonville two weeks after his father.

Tom King – Tom King (ca. 1848 - ?) was possibly the son of Joshua King, blacksmith, according to the 1850 census of New Britain.

Towny – (Feb. 16, 1842 - 1925) Townshend Brandegee, brother of Charles and Robert Bolling Brandegee, grew up on Worthington Ridge near Lyman B.'s grandmother. He also served in the Civil War. Afterwards, he married Katharine Curran in San Diego, CA. He remained in California until his death.

Wadsworth Washburn – (Aug. 15, 1836 – Sep. 17, 1862) He was the son of Rev. Asahel Washburn, minister of the Berlin Congregational Church. Born Aug. 15, 1836 in Royalton, VT, he lived on Worthington Ridge in Berlin. His sister Gertrude married Henry French Norton. Wadsworth enlisted in August, 1862, and was promoted to First Sergeant, 16th Conn., Co. G. He was killed at the Battle of Antietam, Sep. 17, 1862, where fellow soldier Jacob Bauer claimed he was hit with seven bullets. He is now buried in Denison (aka Bridge) Cemetery, Berlin.

Wallace Andrews/Andrus – (ca. 1844 - ?) He grew up in East Berlin, son of George Andrews, a blacksmith. One of his near neighbors was fellow soldier Walter Smith. He enlisted Jul. 30, 1862. He became a first Lieutenant in the 16th Conn., Co. I, and was captured Apr. 20, 1864. He was paroled Feb. 28, 1865. He later married and moved west.

Uncle Walter – Possibly Walter Bulkley (ca. 1823 – May 10, 1862 or 1864), son of Justus and Ruth Bulkley, born in Berlin. He was Lyman B.'s maternal uncle.

Walter Smith – (Nov. 13, 1842 – Sep. 13, 1932) A Berlin resident and fellow soldier of the 16th Conn., Co. G, who enlisted in July, 1862. He was wounded at the Battle of Antietam and captured along with Lyman B. and others at Plymouth, NC. In the 1860 census he is listed as a mechanic living with his parents. He was imprisoned with Lyman B. at Andersonville and paroled with him. Smith is buried in Wilcox Cemetery, East Berlin.

Old Warren – Possibly Albert Warren (1833 – 1904), who lived on Worthington Ridge, Berlin when Lyman B. was a child. He died in 1904 and is buried in Maple Cemetery, Berlin.

Willie Atwood – (ca. 1844 - ?) He lived in western Kensington, CT, possibly on Edgewood Rd.[6] He enlisted in the 15th Conn. Regiment, Co. F on Aug. 25, 1862 and was mustered out Jun. 27, 1865.[7]

Willie Parsons –Possibly J. Willard Parsons (ca. 1844 - 1897) who in 1870 lived next door to Francis and Mary Chambers, Lyman B.'s aunt and uncle. He was a musician. He is buried in Fairview Cemetery, New Britain.

---

[6] 1850 US Census, also Smith's map of Hartford County, 1855

[7] U.S. Civil War Soldiers Records & Profiles, Historical Data Systems, comp.. *U.S. Civil War Soldier Records and Profiles* [database on-line]. Provo, UT, USA: Ancestry.com Operations Inc, 2009.

MAPS
Berlin, CT Map

Ca. 1855 map of Berlin, CT. (1) shows Lyman B.'s first home on Toll Gate Road and (2) shows his second home with his grandmother Ruth Bulkley on Worthington Ridge.

New Britain, CT Map

Ca. 1855 map of New Britain, CT, just north of Berlin. The star notes where Aunt Hattie and Uncle Lester Booth lived. Lyman, Robert and Hattie Wilcox also lived with the Booths for some time.

Map of Engagements

16ᵗʰ Connecticut Volunteer Regiment Map of Engagements

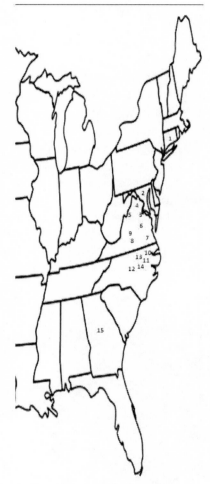

1. The 16ᵗʰ Connecticut Infantry was mustered into service in Hartford, CT
   August 24, 1862
2. Maryland Campaign
   September 6 – 22, 1862
   Battle of Antietam, Sharpsburg, MD
   September 16 – 17, 1862
3. Movement to Falmouth, VA
   October 27 – November 17, 1862
4. Battle of Fredericksburg, VA
   December 12 – 15, 1862
5. Burnside's "Mud March", VA:
   January 20 – 24, 1863
6. Movement to Newport News, VA
   February 6 – 9, 1863
7. Siege of Suffolk, VA
   April 12 – May 4, 1863
8. Action on Edenton Road, VA
   April 24, 1863
   Action at Providence Church and Nansemond River, VA
   May 3, 1863
9. Dix's Peninsula Campaign, VA
   June 27 – July 7, 1863
   Expedition from White House (9) to the South Anna River, VA (10)
   July 1 – 7, 1863
10. Skirmish, Harrellsville, VA
    January 20, 1864
11. Movement to Plymouth, NC
    January 24 – 28, 1864
12. Skirmish, Windsor, NC
    January 30, 1864
13. Siege, Plymouth, NC
    April 17 – 20, 1864
14. Surrender, Plymouth, NC: Almost all of the members of the 16ᵗʰ CT were captured at Plymouth
    April 20, 1864
15. Imprisonment – Andersonville, GA and other southern prisons
    April, 1864 – June 24, 1865

CHAPTER 1
Lyman B. Wilcox: The Early Years

Lyman Bulkley Wilcox (Lyman B.) was born in Berlin, Connecticut on January 20, 1845. He was the son of Lyman Wilcox (Lyman, Sr.) and Maria Bulkley, who were married in Berlin September 26, 1843.[8] He was the oldest of three children born to the couple, having a younger brother Robert (Rob or Robbie), and a younger sister Harriet (Hattie). His family tree contains the names of many old Berlin families, and includes some of the oldest names to settle Farmington, Middletown, and Wethersfield in Connecticut. Some of his forefathers fought in the American Revolution. Others were pioneers in early Berlin industry. Some of the friends and neighbors he mentions in the letters became pillars of the community. Others died on the battlefields, from disease, or in the prison camps.

It is likely that Lyman B. was born in a house his father had recently built on Toll Gate Road.

Lyman B.'s first home on Toll Gate Road, Berlin, Connecticut

---

[8] Berlin Vital Records, 1849-1875

Lyman B. Wilcox: The Early Years

His birth was heralded by his family as a balm to the sorrow of losing Justus Bulkley, Lyman B.'s maternal grandfather, who had died at age 48 the previous year. The following excerpt from an 1859 letter written to Lyman B. by his aunt Harriet Booth describes his dearness to the family:

> *"I cannot tell you, my dear boy, how much happiness your letter gave me. As I read those lines, breathing of affection, my mind ran back over some thirteen years, checkered with gladness and grief, to the time when you, then a rosy little darling, first began to lisp your "baby talk". Do you know, Lyman, the first word ever you said was "Hattie"? Well do I remember my joy, when after many unsuccessful attempts, you at length succeeded in pronouncing it to my satisfaction. Did you ever think, dear Lyman, how much affection we all have for you? You came to us, when we were sitting in the Shadow of your Grandpa's death. In your innocence and helplessness you came, demanding our love and care; our sorrow was, in a measure, buried in a new joy – the joy of your existence. As the first grandchild, the first nephew, you became very near and dear to us. As you grew and began to return our love with your baby caresses, sickness came upon you, and we feared the Shadow was again to brood over us. But a merciful God spared your life, perhaps for some great purpose."*

The family lived in Worthington Parish, Berlin in 1850, on the east side of Toll Gate Road, by a pond and the Tinman Toll Factory along Belcher Brook.[9] His father had learned the trade of 'tintool manufacturer',[10] from his father-in-law, making the tools needed for the working of tin into saleable items such as plates, cups and other utility objects.. Berlin was the birthplace of the original "Yankee Peddler", selling tin products which William and Edward Pattison had made famous along the eastern U.S. as early as 1740. A number of supportive industries were established by the early

---

[9] Smith's Map of Hartford County, 1855, a copy of which is at the Berlin Historical Society Museum. It was originally at the Selden School in Beckley Quarter.
[10] Ibid.

21

and mid-nineteenth century. Some of them later diversified into other areas and still survive to this day.

Belcher Brook from Toll Gate Road, Berlin

A little pocket of industry flourished along Belcher Brook after the American Revolution. Dams created ponds, and the water powered a number of mills for a good part of the nineteenth century. One of these was an enterprise owned by William Kilbourne, who owned a dye house and shop that was sold to Lucius Cook of Wallingford, Connecticut in 1795. The property later sold several times until it came into the hands of Justus Bulkley and his brother William around 1830.[11] They made German silver spoons and silver plated spoons, in addition to tinners' tools. When Justus Bulkley died in 1844, son-in-law Lyman, Sr. bought some of the property. He built a house nearby. Lyman B. spent the first ten years of his life here. The road has a history of being a toll-road, hence the name. A little further north

---

[11] North, p. 238

along Belcher Brook was a shop known as the Blair Factory where, in the early 1800s, James Lamb made an early cookstove. Later, farm implements were made here. One old story states that pikes were made here for John Brown, who might have used them for his Harper's Ferry raid.[12]

The Wilcox family has a long history in Berlin and Middletown, Connecticut, going back to the first settlers in the mid-1600s. John Wilcox, the patriarch and immigrant, came from England and settled first in Hartford with Rev. Thomas Hooker. He later moved and became one of the founders of Middletown. Much of the eastern part of the town of Berlin was originally part of the northwest corner of Middletown, called the Upper Houses. Many of the Wilcox family settled on the western side of the Mattabesset River which, when Berlin was incorporated in 1785, put them in East Berlin.

Lyman B.'s family tree includes other early families, including family names such as Bulkley, Savage, Dickinson, Sage, Beckley, and Gilbert. The town of Berlin in 1850 was composed mainly of Connecticut-born people of English descent. A number of Irish immigrants had begun to settle, often brought in by the advent of the railroad, which the Irish helped to build. Like many of the children of the town, Lyman B. was related to a number of his classmates.

Lyman B.'s first years on Toll Gate Road were probably like most youngsters of the day. Life revolved around school, church, and home. He would have walked to school, which was probably on Worthington Ridge; old maps show a school across from the old meeting house, on the northwest corner of School St. He may also have gone to one of the smaller private schools that were around town. Lyman B. may have, at times, gone to work with his father, in the expectation that he would learn something of the business. The following excerpt from an 1852 letter Lyman, Sr. wrote to his wife, Maria, gives a small taste of seven-year-old Lyman B.'s life:

---

[12] Ibid.,p.246

Field Music: From Antietam to Andersonville

"When I left the Berlin Depot, I was sorry to leave Lyman B. He appear'd to feel bad about something, but what, I do not know. He was so grieved he could not speak, but I suppose he was fearful he should not find the way home."

Lyman B. would also have had a certain amount of chores to do, especially as he was the eldest child. Those tasks might have included chopping and stacking wood, cleaning the barn, and helping to take care of the animals. Most folk at that time had at least a cow and some chickens. Nearly everyone had some sort of a garden for vegetables. Farming was still a major enterprise in town. On Sunday, the whole family went to church. They might have walked, or taken a carriage ride, if they had one. Sunday was a time spent in worship, and then visiting family and friends.

Both of Lyman B.'s grandmothers were still living when he was a child. Grandma Bulkley lived on Worthington Ridge, not too far from the new church, and Grandma Wilcox lived in East Berlin. Lyman B.'s paternal grandfather, another Lyman Wilcox, had died in 1827 at the age of 43, beginning a pattern that would all too soon recur.

Circa 1836 view of Worthington Ridge, Berlin from the north

Lyman B. Wilcox: The Early Years

Lyman, Sr. suffered from asthma, and his letter in 1854 shows the health difficulties he commonly faced:

> *"I shall not be able to write you much at this time and place, that is in this smoke room and in the smoke of two or three hundred foolish men. But perhaps I can better write than talk for if I should attempt to speak, I should take in a volume of folly (smoke) and should be used up for the night. I did not arrive in Springfield till after dark on Tuesday and then had the Asthma very bad all night, so much so that I thought it would not be prudent for me to go any further, but in the morning I felt a little better, but did not start for Boston till noon. After I had got over the asthma I was very tired and sleepy and was soon asleep in the cars."*

Lyman, Sr. died of pneumonia in 1855 at the age of 36, less than a year after writing the above letter. Lyman B. was just ten years old.

Suddenly, his world was turned upside-down. There was not enough money. Land was sold, and eventually Maria Wilcox and her three children moved from the Toll Gate Road house to Worthington Ridge to live with Maria's mother, Ruth Bulkley. The benefits to this were that school was closer, and there were plenty of friends around. Lyman B. was right down the street from the Brandegee boys, Charlie, Rob and Townshend ("Towney"), and others were close by.

The loss of the father must have been devastating to the young family. Whether the dying process was long or short, to a ten-year-old it was life changing. In the nineteenth century, though, it was all too common. Without antibiotics and modern medical advances, communicable diseases took a heavy toll.

Fate had not finished with this family, however, for three years later, Lyman B.'s mother Maria fell victim to consumption, known today as tuberculosis. During most of the nineteenth century and even early into the twentieth century, tuberculosis was one of the most common causes of death in Berlin. It did not discriminate; it took the young, the poor and the wealthy, and sometimes decimated entire households.

Graves of Lyman B.'s parents, Lyman Wilcox, Sr. and Maria Bulkley Wilcox in Wilcox Cemetery, East Berlin, CT

Grandma Bulkley became guardian to Lyman B., Rob, and Hattie. She did her best to provide love and guidance to the three orphans, and Maria's two sisters, Aunts Hattie and Mary, also played a big part in their lives. Aunt Hattie in particular felt very close to her nephew, as her letter from April 15, 1859 shows.

"But a merciful God spared your life, perhaps for some great purpose. He spared you, but he has seen fit to deprive you of a father's counsel and a mother's prayers. But he has not left you comfortless. You have a dear brother and sister and many friends... I often think, how happy we ought to be, because we feel so well assured that those dear ones are left in a heavenly

> *hand… I often think of them as wandering hand in hand; with the smile of God's countenance resting ever upon them…Let us try to live, my dear boy, so that when our summons come, we too, may go forth with gladness and singing, and sorrow and sighing shall flee away forever."*

Lyman B. was thirteen by this time, and old enough to start preparing for manhood. From April to October in 1859 he went to Branford, Connecticut to work on his cousin Samuel Fowler's farm. A number of letters written back and forth demonstrate the closeness of family members. In the following letter to his grandmother Ruth Bulkley, Lyman B. lists what he has learned on the farm and mentions missing home:

> *Branford Apr 29ᵗʰ /59*
> *Dear Grandma*
> *I have just received your letter of the 26ᵗʰ and was very glad to hear from home as I always am. I suppose that you are cleaning house now and are very busy. We have just began to do our spring work and I have had to work every day since I have been here. I try to be contented but can't help thinking of home sometimes and wishing I was there. I have learned a great deal so quick. I can plough, drive team, fodder cattle, and a great many other things. I have had the toothache two or three times but have not had to use the Mustard. Tell Robbie I have put a mast, bowsprit, jib-boom, boom, gaff, topmast and two or three ropes on my boat. I have not got time to write to Robbie now for I must write to Henry. But I guess I will write a little to Aunt Polly. Aunt Hattie has sent me three or four letters and a paper. I suppose their party was a grand affair at your house. Aunt Hattie told me all about it. But I think I must bid you <u>Bon Repos</u> (good night).*
> > *I remain your*
> > *aff Grandson*
> > *Lyman*

Field Music: From Antietam to Andersonville

The following letter, written by 10 year old Robbie in April, 1859 to Lyman B. in Branford, is transcribed exactly as written, retaining its youthful mistakes.

MY. DEAR. BROTHER.
I. SHOULD. LIKE. TO. KNOW. HOW. YOU. GET. A. LONG. I. HAVE. BEEN. OVER. ON. ~~MOUNT.LAMENTATION~~ THE. MOUNTING. CHARLY AND. TOWNY. TIM. AND. ARTHUR. WE. HAD. PRETTY. GOOD. TIMES. BUT. ARTHUR. CRIDE. BE.CAUSE. HE. GOT. TIRED. I. HAVE. GOT. MY. RABBIS. [rabbits] UNCLE. FRANK. IS A. GOING. TO. HELP. ME. I. WENT. OVER. TO. THE. DEPOT. election day and the rest of the boys AND. SEE. SOME. SOLDIERS. THEY. LOOKED. NICE. IN. THAT. APPLE. TREE. OVER. IN. THE. CHURCH. YARD. WHERE. YOU. GOT. YOUR. BLUEBIRD'S. EGG. THERE. IS. A. BLUEBIRD'S. NEST. WITH. 5. EGGS. IN. IT. UNCLE. WALTER. WAS. UP. HERE. SUNDAY. AND. LARK. [a horse] HAD. A. FIT. AND. DIED. I. FELT. VERY. BAD. I. THINK. YOU. WILL. FEEL. VERY. SORRY. UNCLE. WALTER. HAD. BROUGHT. HER. A. MUZZLES. SO. SHE. COULD. NOT. BITE. ANY. BODY. I. AM. VERY. SORRY. THAT. JIM. CANNOT. GET. YOU. ANY. RINGS. HATTY. AND. ME. SEND. 9999. KISSES. TO. YOU. HATTY. IS. VERY. WELL. I. HAD. AN. AWFUL. TOOTH. ACHE. THI. MORNING. WE. ALL. SEND. OUR. LOVE. TO. YOU. I. WAS. VERY. GLAD. TO. RECEIVE. YOUR. JOURNAL. PLEASE. EXCUSE. ALL. THE. BLOTS.
GOOD. BYE.
FROM. ROB.

Mentions of Mount Lamentation must have made Lyman B. homesick. The mountain gets its name from an old tale of a Mr. Chester of Wethersfield who got lost on the way to New Haven, back in the seventeenth century, when most of Connecticut was still a wilderness. (Happily he was found and made a full recovery.) Robbie also mentioned Election Day; at that time elections were held in the springtime.

Drawing by Lyman B. on an envelope sent to Robbie

Lyman B. and Robbie were particularly close and wrote many letters to each other while Lyman was away in Branford. The following two excerpts from Lyman B.'s letters display some of their closeness:

From June 16, 1859
"I suppose you are getting along nicely at home and I would give a great deal to be with you. Samuel and me intend to go to New Haven the 4ᵗʰ of July for they are going to have great times there, just think to spend <u>One Thousand Dollars</u> for fireworks. I suppose your Rabbits are well. Please let me know all about them in your next letter. I hope you will take good care of "Screamer" for I shall want to rig her up again when I come home...
Don't get hurt for I feel worried about you sometimes. I guess I shall come home for a short time in August as we don't have much to do then..."

From October, 1859
"Hurrah Rob

> *Here comes the last letter from Branford I hope. I guess I shall come the 15ᵗʰ and shan't I be glad to "get out the wilderness".*

> *I think I shall go to the State Fair in New Haven and I hope you and Grandma will come. Samuel says he thinks you had ought to, and I think so too. You ask Grandma if she want go to the fair and if she says no, I would advise you to cry 'till she says yes..."*

Not long after returning from Branford, in 1860 or 1861, Lyman B. spent time in New Britain, Connecticut with his Aunt Hattie and Uncle Lester Booth, a shoemaker. He lived in New Britain in 1862 prior to enlisting in the Army.

During the pre-war years abolitionist sentiment was growing in town. The attack on Fort Sumter spurred enlistments, and Lyman B., like many youths, became enamored of the soldier's life. It was in his blood. Lyman B. was a great grandson of Seth Savage, a veteran of the American Revolution, who died only three years before he was born. Lyman B. would have grown up hearing tales of his ancestor's exploits from his grandmother, Ruth Savage Bulkley. A paternal great-grandfather, Josiah Wilcox, was a fifer in the Revolutionary army.[13] Another ancestor, Nathaniel Dickinson, saw action, which included the burning of Danbury in 1777 and the invasion of New Haven in 1779.[14] Yet another ancestor, Great Grandfather Justus Bulkley, Sr., had worked with Simeon North in his pistol factory on Spruce Brook in Berlin.[15] North was reputed to be the best pistol maker in the country. His innovation of making gun parts interchangeable won him a contract with the U.S. government in 1808. His contributions helped win the War of 1812. Patriotism was

---

[13] Adams, p.752

[14] Heritagequest Online Revolutionary War Pension Applications, Series M805, Roll268, Image 584, File W25540

[15] North, p.33

something that was inbred in Lyman B., and he was eager to do his duty.

Grave of Josiah Wilcox, Wilcox Cemetery, East Berlin, CT

At some point Lyman B. learned how to play the drum, as evidenced by the following letter sent to him:

> *Boston Dec 4 / 1861*
> *Mr. Wilcox*
>   *Dr Sir*
>   *We have lately issued a new edition of the "Modern Drum School" which contains in addition to former matter all the Drum & Fife Music used in the military service as well as the Bugle Calls for Infantry and skirmishes, according to the U.S. Manual. Price 75c. There is no other similar book we know of.*
>   *Respectfully*
>   *Oliver Dixson & Co*
>   *Berger*

Field Music: From Antietam to Andersonville

It is not clear from his letters if he hid this skill from his grandmother, but it is obvious he did not want her to know he was learning the marching tunes. Lyman B. wrote to Robbie in one letter between 1861 and 1862:

> *"And Rob please bring up those "drum sticks" will you, and be pretty sly about it as I don't want any one to see them."*

By March, 1862, Lyman B. obviously sought to join the military over his Grandma Bulkley's objection, as shown in the following March 27th letter written to Robbie:

> *"Have they heard from Charlie yet. I have not since I came up the last time. Tell Grandma that she need not trouble herself about getting me a place. I had rather get one myself and then I may be suited. By- Chamberlain has written to his brother Val- and we shall probably hear from him in two or three weeks. And Charlie has offered me a place in his Reg. either as Drummer or Private just as I please. So you see that there is no need of any one in our family troubling themselves about me, especially when I can get a place so easy."*

Lyman B., at the age of 17, finally secured his grandmother's consent. On August 13, 1862, he enlisted, and joined the 16th Connecticut Volunteer Infantry Regiment (16th Conn.) as a musician for Co. G. He spent the next few days in Hartford, before the regiment mustered on Aug. 24th. He was now a soldier.

Records from the Berlin Town Clerk's Office, showing Lyman B.'s enlistment

32

Chapter 2
The Maryland Campaign

In 1862, President Lincoln, in an effort to fortify the U.S. Army and end the Civil War, called for three hundred thousand volunteers to serve in the Union Army for three years. The 16th Connecticut Volunteer Infantry was one of the many regiments formed as a result.

The 16th Conn. was organized in Hartford, Connecticut in the summer of 1862. It was comprised predominantly of men from local counties, with some of the oldest families represented within its ranks. The 16th Conn. was officially mustered into service on August 24, 1862 with 1,007 enlisted men and officers and companies representing Connecticut towns as follows:

Company A – *Hartford and Wethersfield*
Company B – *East Windsor, Guilford, Hartford, and Windsor*
Company C – *Farmington, Hartford, and Rocky Hill*
Company D – *Enfield and Suffield*
Company E – *Canton, Granby, and Simsbury*
Company F – *Hartford*
Company G – *Berlin, East Windsor, Farmington, and Hartford*
Company H – *Bolton, Glastonbury, Manchester, and South
        Windsor*
Company I – *Avon, Stafford, Vernon, and Willington*
Company K – *Bristol, Burlington, and Farmington*

By August 28th, the regiment had been fully equipped and loaded, except for muskets. They were inspected by their Colonel. Records recall that it was a particularly hot day and many of the new soldiers fainted under the heavy loads they now carried. It was a lesson learned for many of the men and a taste of what was to follow.

Ct. State Cap   1991-000-069

A new embroidered color was ordered for the 16th Conn. in 1864. It was not delivered to the Regiment until May, 1865, one month after the war ended. This flag is currently displayed at the State of Connecticut Capitol, Hartford, CT.

On August 29, 1862, the regiment was ordered to Washington, DC. The soldiers left Hartford on August 29th at 3 p.m. via two boats, "City of Hartford" and "Geo. O. Collins", sailing down the Connecticut River to New York City. From there they took the steamer "Kill von Kull" to Elizabeth, New Jersey, then proceeded by train to Baltimore, Maryland and finally arrived in Washington, DC, where the regiment joined the Army of the Potomac.

By September 7, 1862, the 16th Conn. was on the march. The war became a reality for the newly assembled regiment as they encountered many more regiments, ambulances, and injured soldiers along their path. The marching was hard and fast. Rations were few, forcing many men to rely on local farmers for a time. Entering Virginia and then Maryland, the Regiment loaded its muskets for the first time around September 15. As they continued their march, the signs of fierce battle became evident to the novice volunteers of the 16th Conn. as they passed houses and churches riddled with bullets and filled with wounded soldiers. Dead bodies lined the roadways.

On September 16, 1862, the 16th Conn. received a surprising order, calling them to the front line for its first engagement: the Battle of Antietam at Sharpsburg, Maryland. Placed on the flank of the Union line in a cornfield, this regiment, not yet one month in existence, encountered a surprise attack from a very seasoned Confederate division under the leadership of General A. P. Hill. Volley after volley in quick succession was fired into their midst. Of the 779 16th Conn. Volunteers who engaged in this battle, 43 were killed and 161 wounded, with total casualties amounting to 204.

According to fellow Co. G soldier Jacob Bauer, they received guns (old Springfield Rifles) with 40 rounds of ammunition only two days before the Battle of Antietam. They learned how to use a bayonet AFTER the battle. This helps explain why the regiment suffered such heavy casualties during the battle.

Lyman B. started writing his letters home while still in Connecticut.

August 19, 1862
Camp Williams *[probably in Hartford, CT, to Robert Wilcox]*

My very dear brother,
Having a little spare time this morning I thought I would improve it by writing to you. I am now lying down in my tent trying to write with a very poor (lead) pencil. We have just got through Breakfast and Squad drill. You may come up as soon as you can but I hardly think you had better stay over night as you would not enjoy it very much. You can come up with Uncle Frank in the morning, stay all day and go down with him at night. I am enjoying myself very well and don't want to have you feel bad about my going at all. I will write to you often and you must to

me. I have not drawn my drum yet but probably shall to day. Tell Grandma to hurry up my things as soon as possible.

Yours in haste,

Lyman B.

   Love to all the good folks at home

September 3, 1862

Camp near Arlington Heights *[in Virginia, to Ruth Bulkley]*

My dear Grandma

   I hope you will excuse me for not writing to you before, but I have not had hardly a moment's spare time until this afternoon. We left Hartford on Friday Afternoon and arrived at our present encampment Monday night passing through New York, Harrisburg, Baltimore and Washington on our way. I think by this time that I have seen at least a part of this world having seen New York. The Great Eastern. The place where the Massachusetts boys were killed in Baltimore. The capital of this Great American Nation and also that great man Gen. Mc'Clellan, and a big man he is too though he looked pretty rusty when I saw him. He passed by our Regiment just as we were leaving Washington, saluted us, and was out of sight in less than two minutes.

   When we got onto the ground of our present encampment, it was almost 5 o'clock in the evening and we had hardly halted before it began to rain like "blases" and in less than two hours we were all wet through to our skins and by some mistake our tents had not arrived and we had to sleep out on the open ground without even a tree or bush over us. I suppose you will think we did not sleep much that night, but honestly, I think I never slept better in my life then I did that night in the rain. Our tents have not arrived yet, but probably will some time this week. **Walter Smith** and **Wallace Andrews** have been sick, some, since they have been here, but are better now. You need not think I am going to be sick for I am as strong and healthy as can be and there is not the least danger of getting sick if I can take care of myself. I like this kind of life very well indeed and I am sorry you did not let me enlist before.

Our camp is situated about 12 miles from Washington and 4 miles from Arlington Heights. We are also about 3 miles from Alexandria and Fairfax Court House. The rebels are only a few miles from us and we can see their pickets quite distinctly. Gen's Mc'Dowell, Segiel [Sedgwick], Mc'Clellan and Burnside with their forces are between us and them. I think that our present encampment will be the next battle ground and we shall probably leave for Washington if it is.

Statue of Gen. Sedgwick on the State Capitol Building, Hartford, CT

But I can not write any more at present though there is a great deal that I want to tell you. I will write to Aunt Mary as soon as I can.
Yours Affy,
Lyman B.

Direct your letters to
> Lyman B. Wilcox
> Company G. 16th Regiment C.T.
> Washington. D.C.

Smith, *Walter E.; Private, Company G; Residence, Berlin, Connecticut; Enlisted July 30, 1862; Mustered August 24, 1862; Wounded, Antietam, MD, September 17, 1862; Captured at Plymouth, NC, April 20, 1864; Paroled December 10, 1864; Discharged May 27, 1865.*

Andrews (Andrus), *Wallace R.; 1st Lieutenant, Company I; Residence, Berlin, Connecticut; Enlisted July 30, 1862; Mustered August 24, 1862; Captured at Plymouth, NC, April 20, 1864; Paroled February 28, 1865; Discharged May 15, 1865.*

Undated letter, Probably September 13, 1862
Camp near Arlington Heights, Saturday noon. *[in Virginia]*

My very dear Grandma,
We have just received orders to be ready to march tomorrow morning without knapsacks and with 40 rounds of cartridges to each man. So not knowing when I may have another chance to write to you, I thought I would improve the present opportunity and let you know where we are agoing to. The company officers say that we are agoing to Leesburg, a distance of 30 miles from here, but they probably do not know much about it. At any rate it is pretty evident that we are to see some fighting, and if we do fight, you may expect that the "bully 16th" will give a good account of themselves. We all appear to be in first rate spirits

from the "Colonel" down to "Drummer Boy". I have been a little unwell for the last day or two (on account of the water probably) but I feel better already now and shall probably be all right tomorrow. I have not received any letters from home yet, but I hope I shall before I leave here. You can direct all your letters as before that is to

> Lyman B. Wilcox
> Co. G. 16th Regiment, CT
> Washington,
> D.C.

I have written 3 letters since I have been here which probably have been received by this time. You need not feel at all concerned about my being sick for I have not felt really sick at all, only a <u>little</u> unwell.

Please give my love to all and reserve a good share for yourself. Tell Aggie that her Bible is worth more to me than all the other things in my knapsack and I can never thank her half enough for it. I wish you and the rest would write to me as soon as you can.

> Yours in haste
> Lyman B.

September 20, 1862
Hospital near Boones "boro" [*Boonsboro*], Maryland

My dear Grandma and the other dear friends at home.

Thinking you might be rather anxious to hear from me after the battle I have taken the opportunity this morning to write you a few lines.

I came out of the battle without being hurt at all and that is what most of our boys cannot say.

I have not written to you before because when we got to Washington on our way out here, our Knapsacks were taken away from us and we were only allowed to carry an "overcoat" and blanket with us and so of course we have not any writing materials with us. The only way that I can write now is by taking a leaf out of my Memorandum Book and when it is written I do not know how I shall send it. I have not as yet received any letters at all from home, but I suppose there is a plenty of them waiting for me at Washington.

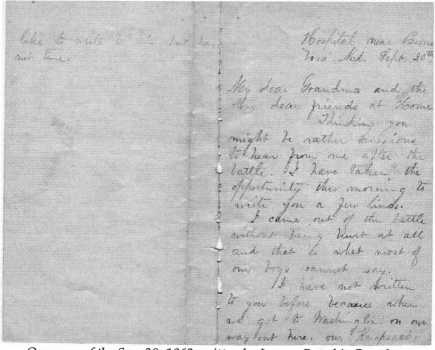

One page of the Sep. 20, 1862 written by Lyman B. to his Grandma

In the last battle of ours I was detailed for Hospital service or I should have most certainly have been killed or wounded with the rest of the boys.

Wadsworth Washburn and **Ed Parmalee** were killed and eight others from our company but no other Berlin boys.

I cannot tell you where to direct your letters to as we are moving all of the while.

Give my love to all of the dear good folks at home.

And believe me your aff. Nephew,
    Lyman B. Wilcox

Give my love most especially to Rob and tell him I should like to write to him but have not time.

Washburn, *Wadsworth A.; 1st Sergeant, Company G; Residence, Berlin, Connecticut; Enlisted August 8, 1862; Mustered August 24, 1862; Killed in Action, Antietam, Maryland, September 17, 1862.*

Parmelee, *Edward A.; Sergeant, Company G; Residence, Hartford, Connecticut; Enlisted July 25, 1862; Mustered August 24, 1862; Killed in Action, Antietam, Maryland, September 17, 1862.*

Monument commemorating the 16ᵗʰ Conn. Volunteer Infantry at the Antietam Battleground, Sharpsburg, Maryland

October 6, 1862
Camp near Sharpsburg, Md.

My dear Brother Robbie,
As Fred Nettleton was going home I thought I would improve the opportunity and send you a few little things.

In the first place I send you my Testament thinking perhaps that you would like to see an Army Testament and I can get a plenty more. I hope you will read it often for my sake. I also send you some "Laish" Cartridges which I picked up behind the rebel brestworks the day after the battle. One of them you will see is the "Famed" Ball and three buck-shot.

The one that is knocked up so is a ball that was fired at our men. Wether it hit any one or not I cannot say.

Besides these I send you a sample of our hard bread or "hard tack" as the boys call it. It is not near as bad as some that we have had, but I think you will say that it is not very good ~~for a steady~~ to live on entirely.

Fred has also got some iron ore that we picked up near our camp. He will give you a piece of it I guess.

I do not know but these things will get pretty well smashed up before you get them but I believe it is the best chance I shall have to send you anything.

If you wish to know how we live down here, Fred will inform you as he has tented with me ever since we have been here and knows the whole thing. However don't believe to many of his stories as he may try to stuff you a little.

I am very well now and am waiting quite impatiently to hear from you. I have not heard for a long while. Mr. Washburn was here last night and brought me a bundle from Grandma which I was very glad indeed to get.

I should like to hear from Uncle Lester occasionally, and I hope that Aunt Hattie will write as often as she can. Give my love to all of them and accept a good share yourself. Excuse all mistakes as I have had to scribble this off in a great hurry.
Write soon.

Your affectionate brother,
Lyman

And Rob I have really seen old Lincoln. He reviewed our division the other day and with him was Burnside and Mc'Clellan.

Lincoln looked especially like old Warren only his face was thinner and whiter.

Don't have too much to do with Fred Nettleton and don't for heavens sake have <u>anything</u> to do with Tom King.

Tell Lyman and Mike that shoemaking is all played out and that they had right to be down here where all of the "big folks" live.

Yours in hopes of seeing you soon
Lyman B. Wilcox

President Abraham Lincoln at Antietam, Maryland on October 3, 1862, to review the troops and encourage General McClellan to pursue and attack the Confederate Army

Chapter 3
Pleasant Valley, Maryland to Suffolk, Virginia

The 16th Conn. Regiment left the Sharpsburg, Maryland area on October 7, 1863, marching less than 10 miles to Pleasant Valley, Maryland. The march, though short, was a difficult one, with narrow paths, heavy loads, and a rocky climb. At the camp at Pleasant Valley, the regiment suffered severely from exhaustion and illness, with few men able to march again for a period of time.

From Pleasant Valley, the 16th Conn. fell in on October 28, 1863 for another march, ultimately culminating in Falmouth, Virginia. Again the conditions were difficult. The men marched many miles a day, with harsh weather conditions prevailing, limited rations, and some men without shoes. The enemy was close by throughout the march. Despite these difficulties, the Regiment marched 175 miles in 12 days.

Encampment in Falmouth proved little better. The terrain was flat. Torrential rains left standing water, creating mud inches deep. Fires could not be built, tents could not be raised, and rations were scant. This encampment is sometimes known as Camp Starvation or Starvation Hollow.

The 16th Conn. next saw battle in Fredericksburg, Virginia. On the morning of December 11, they woke to the sound of artillery fire. Now under the command of General Burnside, the Regiment was still not combat ready, only being in service less than four full months. They were ordered to advance, but luckily orders then changed to hold them in reserve. They watched the battle rage for three days and were placed in a position to make an assault against the Confederate position, which General Burnside called off at the last minute. This move saved the ranks of the 16th Conn., since the Fredericksburg battle was a considerable defeat for the Union forces.

Pleasant Valley, Maryland to Suffolk, Virginia

The Regiment remained in the Fredericksburg area for several weeks, with drilling, preparation for marching, and picket duty being the chief occupations during this time. The conditions of the camp were poor, with continued bad weather and poor quarters causing sickness and death, dwindling the ranks.

The 16th Conn. next saw action in what is now known as Burnside's Second Campaign – the "Mud March", January 20-24, 1863. General Burnside's plan to cross the Rappahannock River and surprise the Confederates was thwarted by an unseasonably warm January, leading to considerable mud along the river. The mud made the passing of troops and artillery impossible, thus ending the planned attack. This was the second and last of Burnside's campaigns in the Civil War.

On February 6, 1863, the 16th Conn. connection with the Army of the Potomac was dissolved and they were ordered to Newport News and then Suffolk, Virginia. They were ultimately aligned to the Department of Virginia. This was a period of rebuilding for the Regiment, with several recruits joining them during this time.

October 26, 1862
Camp at Plesant Valley [Maryland]

My very dear brother,
I have changed my mind about the "Pipe" business that I wrote about the other day and I think that I shall be able to get along without smoking for some time longer and therefore I think that you need not send the pipe. I suppose you will be somewhat surprised to get a letter from me so soon but not knowing when I should have another chance to write I thought I would improve the present opportunity. Saturday night we were ordered to be ready in full marching order and with two days rations to march at 9 o'clock Sunday morning.

So agreeable to said orders we turned out in the midst of a pouring rain and stood in line for two hours when we were

45

marched back to our company streets and dismissed for the present but to hold ourselves in readiness to march at a moments notice. So we went into our tents and lay down and how the rain poured down our little tents affording us scarcely any protection from it. Such a Sunday you never saw and I hope never will. We lay in the wet all night and I can say that I slept very well but all my dreams were of home and when I came to awake and find out where I was, it was slightly discouraging I must say. However this (Monday) morning the sun has come out bright but not very warm and we are all in good spirits once more. I do not think we shall leave to day but shall probably go tomorrow morning early. Where we are agoing to I cannot say but probably not very far from our present position.

We may be going into "winter quarters" but it is more likely that we shall go over into "ole Varginny" again.

I hope you will write as soon as you can for I can get yours as well if we do march. Direct to Washington D.C. as usual. I received all of those papers that you sent me and I return my sincere thanks for them.

If you have a chance to send me any thing by Henry Porter or other folks coming on this way. I wish if it would be no trouble to you to send me some of that chocolate. You know which I mean, it comes in little square cakes, You used to get it when you came to New Britain to see me. It will be one of the best things that you can send me if you can get it. The boys use it on the march and one of the best things about it is that it only takes a minute to fix it. We just set a cup full of water on the fire which becomes hot in a few moments and then putting a piece of the chocolate in it we have a good hot cup of chocolate already sweetened in a very short space of time.

I wish that I had more time to write you but I must try to get this in before the mail closes. I will write again as soon as possible. Excuse all mistakes and believe me as your

Aff Brother,

Lyman B. Wilcox

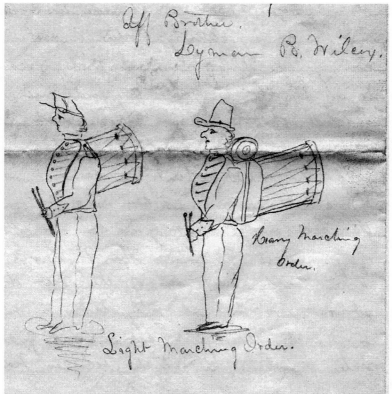

Drawing by Lyman B. in his Oct. 26, 1862 letter, showing the difference in packing for a 'Light Marching Order' vs. a 'Heavy Marching Order'

November 11, 1862
Camp near Warrenton, Va.

My very dear brother

Having nothing else to do at present I thought I would improve the opportunity to write you a few lines though I do not know as I shall ever have an opportunity to send them to you as our mail does not run now we are in an enemy's country. That is we are allowed to receive letters but can rarely send them.

We are now stopping at a place called Warrenton waiting for rations. We are only about sixty miles from "Richmond" and

47

thirty from "Washington" and about forty or fifty from "Harpers Ferry". I do not know what our army is trying to do this campaign but I should think that it was intended for a movement on Richmond but still it hardly looks like it either now, as our whole army is now lying still and old "Burnside" has gone to Washington on business I suppose. There has been a report around camp lately that the 8th, 11th and 16th Regiments were to do guard duty at the Rail-road about five or six miles from here and I hope that it is true as we shall have a "bully time" then and may have a chance to get some things from home which I very much need. I will send you a <u>list</u> if I see any chance of getting any thing through.

And now Rob I want to tell you my adventures on the march. In the first place we left our encampment at Harpers Ferry about the first of the month I believe and began our tramp and we have been on the walk nearly ever since. Awful hard walking too. I thought more than once that I should have to give out. But as I had stood it ever since I have been out here with out giving out it went awfully against the grain. But one morning when I got up I found myself very weak indeed and troubled greatly with the Dysentery but I took up the march with the rest and made out to keep along with the Reg. until late in the afternoon when I gave out with sheer exhaustion. I fell out with **Mr. Tibbals** of East Berlin who was about as badly off as I was. We lay right down where we fell until all the Division had marched past us when being rested a little we got up and tried to go along again but could proceed far without resting. We had not been away from the Reg. more than 15 minutes when along comes the Provost Guard and Rob for the first time in my life I was under guard.

But you need not think that there is any disgrace in it, for it is not considered so out here there was a Quartermaster, a first lieutenant and a 2nd lieutenant under guard also besides 20 or 30 men and Tibbals and myself.

Grave of Henry Tibbals in Wilcox Cemetery, East Berlin, CT

We were only kept under guard for a day or two and were treated first rate and were then returned to our Regiments with the caution not to leave them again if we could possibly keep up. I will tell you more particulars about it when I see you again which I hope will be soon, don't you. When we were out only about a week from Harpers Ferry we were treated to a regular old fashioned snow-storm and I think that the weather was some degrees colder than I ever saw in Conn, especially at this time of the year and then to crown all of our troubles we were marched from early in the morning until ten o'clock at night, so you can imagine that we were about played out when we did stop. To avoid falling out this day I was obliged to abandon my drum which made me feel rather bad, but it was pretty badly smashed up and one head gone, so I did not care quite so much not being able to get it fixed out here. I shall draw another from our Quartermaster as soon as possible.

We have been stopping at our present incampment for a day or two now and are getting quite rested. I am enjoying very good health at present and I do not think I shall be obliged to fall out again.

Tibbals, *Henry; Corporal, Company G; Residence, Berlin, Connecticut; Enlisted August 8, 1862; Mustered August 24, 1862; Captured at Plymouth, NC, April 20, 1864; Died in prison, Andersonville, GA, July 31, 1864.*

November 14, 1862
Camp of 16th Reg. CT at Warrenton, Va.

My very dear Rob,

    I suppose you would rather receive an old letter than not any at all and so I think I will send along the foregoing scribble. I commenced it a day or two ago not knowing as I should ever have a chance to send it to you but the report is that a mail leaves for Washington tomorrow morning and so I think I will have this ready to send on. There is still no signs of us moving from here and I think it is on account of the change of Generals in our army. What do you think of the removal of Mc'Clellan. The boys in our Division seem very well satisfied with it and they think that something will be done now that Burnside can have a swing at the Reb's. Our Burnside as the boys in our brigade call him. I suppose you know that we are in his favorite brigade – the one that he took down to New bern with him on that famous expedition to against Fort Macon. Our official position is --- 16th Regiment, C.T. 2nd Brigade, 3rd Division, 9th Army Corps.

    Burnside, before he took Mc'Clellan's place, commanded the 2nd, 9th, and 12th Army Corps. I suppose he now commands the entire army of the Potomac.

    The only fault any of the boys found with little Mc' was that he was to slow and cautious. Now if he had followed up the victory of Antietam, he might have prevented the enemy from crossing the Potomac and captured the whole lot as they acknowledged themselves.

I have received your Bully good letter of the 2nd and you can imagine that I was not sorry to get it. Though I did not like the news from the 14th so well. I expect that "surprise party" of yours was a big thing was it not and I am glad that you have got acquainted with the boys and girls so well and I think you have chosen a first rate set for your acquaintances.

New Britain aint such a very bad place after all is it. I have not seen any that I have liked much better and you may travel the whole world over and I hardly think you will.

I suppose you will begin to go to school before long and you will not have so much work to do then, but I hope you will do all in your power to help Uncle Lester as you will never find a better place in this world. I am very sorry that I did not do better while I was there as I shall probably never get so good a place again, even if I get out of the army all right.

I think I should be willing to work the ends of my fingers off if I could enjoy the privileges that I did before enlisting. However I make out to enjoy myself after a certain fashion and as well as the majority of the men I guess though I am sorely puzzled how to pass away my time very often. All kinds of reading matter and especially papers command a high premium and I hope you will lose no opportunity to send on any thing in that shape. Please write soon and often and remember me as your aff Brother.

Lyman B. Wilcox

January 24, 1863
Camp Hartford near Fredericksburg *[Virginia]*

My dear Aunt Mary,

I received your very welcome letter of the 19th last evening and my time being mostly unoccupied today I think I will improve a part of it by writing to you. I received Robbie's letter yesterday morning and the money all safe.

I think you are mistaken about our army crossing the Rappahannock. We made the attempt some days ago but were obliged to come back as the roads were so muddy that our Artillery could not be moved. If we could only have got across we should have whipped the Reb's badly as they did not know of the movement and were taking them at a place at which they were not fortified. Robbie wrote me some days ago about **Charlie Brandegee**'s return to his Regiment and I have been trying for the last five or six days to find out where he was encamped but I have not been able to. I have not heard from him since I wrote to him about a month ago but I am in hopes of hearing soon. Letters to him would have to be directed to Washington the same as mine are.

I have not received my box yet and I have given up all hope of seeing it. The man that we sent by to Washington was for some reason or other unable to get it and I do not know when we shall have another chance to send. I am very sorry indeed as I have been reckoning considerably on that <u>box</u>. Now I will try to answer your questions. You wish to know, first, if we have enough to eat. If one could get our full rations we should have a plenty to eat, but full rations are a thing we never get. One day we are short on our beans and the next we are entirely out of Potatoes. Then some days we are given Salt Pork in the place of fresh meat and for the last week or two we have been almost entirely out of Salt, Vinegar, Candles and Molasses. We average about one meal a day, never more than that and it is very well cooked what there is of it. We have for breakfast, a small cup of Coffee and Hard Bread, nothing else, without me are fortunate enough to have the cash. If we have that we can buy of our Salter at quite a reasonable price. Fresh Bread, Cakes, Butter, Milk, Cheese Pies &c. Our next meal is usually between three and four in the afternoon thus answering for both Dinner and Supper. It usually consists of either boiled beans, Fresh Meat soup or Cold Boiled Pork, varied occasionally with Boiled Rice without any Molasses or Sugar. I suppose it is very good fodder but I should have turned up my nose at it at home. I am afraid if I should offer Rob a plate of our Scrip he would think he was insulted. It greatly resembles a mess that Grandma used to fix up for our pig. We have very funny weather down here. It is considerably like the weather we have in Conn. in April. It has not snowed but twice yet this winter but it rains very often and the roads and every where else is awful muddy.

This part of the country is a great deal more plesant in the winter than it is in Conn. but in the summer I should much rather be at home. **Henry Savage** was in my tent yesterday morning and he said that he had just heard from his Father and that he intends coming on there within a week or two.

If he does not come before you receive this letter I wish you would please be so kind as to ask Grandma to send me by him a few postage stamps and some reading matter if she can without any inconvenience and whatever else she is a mind to. It is impossible to get any postage stamps out here at any price, and this is the last one that I have and it is so dirty that I am almost afraid it will not pass. I have carried it ever since the battle of Antietam not sending it because it was so dirty. But I am obliged to send it now or not write at all.

I must close now and get ready for Dress Parade. Please write to me as often as convenient. And remember me as your Aff Nephew.

Lyman B. Wilcox

Give my love to all the dear folks at home and accept a good share yourself. I hope Grandma will send the Postage stamps as soon as possible as I have three or four letters to answer.

Brandegee, Charles; Private, New York 5th Infantry Regiment, Company I; Residence, Berlin, Connecticut; Enlisted January 11, 1862; Transferred to New York 146th Infantry Regiment, Co. A May 4, 1863; Captured at The Wilderness 1864; Mustered out January 11, 1865.

Savage, Henry; Private, Company G; Residence, Berlin, Connecticut; Enlisted July 20, 1862; Mustered August 24, 1862; Promoted to Full Sergeant September 17, 1862; Captured at Plymouth, NC, April 20, 1864; Mustered out June 24, 1865.

Field Music: From Antietam to Andersonville

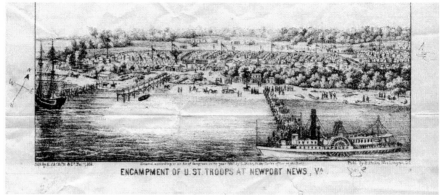

ENCAMPMENT OF U.ST.TROOPS AT NEWPORT NEWS, VA

Letterhead of Lyman B.'s Mar. 9, 1863 letter

March 9, 1863
Newport News *[Virginia]*

My very dear Robbie
    I take the liberty of sending this for your Museum if you want it. That first flag at No. 1 is where our Barracks are situated. No. 2 is where we landed. And that first house at the end of the wharf is our Provost Marshall's.
    Give my love to all the dear folks and reserve a good share for yourself and please remember me as your

Aff Brother,
Lyman B. Wilcox

There is a large gap in letters from Lyman B. to his family from March to June, 1863. During this time, the 16th Conn. participated in the Siege of Suffolk, VA, April 12 to May 4, when the Union Army repelled the Confederate attempt to capture the Federal garrison there. They saw action at Edenton Road, Providence Church and the Nansemond River, VA during the Siege. The following is the only existing letter from Lyman B. Wilcox in this period. Many others never reached their destination.

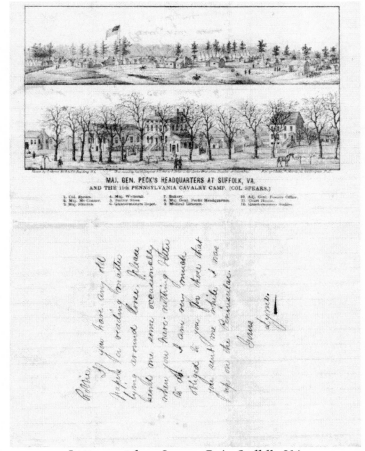

MAJ. GEN. PECK'S HEADQUARTERS AT SUFFOLK, VA.
AND THE 11th PENNSYLVANIA CAVALRY CAMP. (COL. SPEARS.)

Letter sent from Lyman B. in Suffolk, VA

The undated letter reads:

Robbie,

If you have any old papers or reading matter lying around loose, please send me some occasionally when you have nothing better to do. I am very much obliged to you for those that you sent me while I was up on the Peninsular.

Yours,

<u>Lyme.</u>

Chapter 4
Summer in Portsmouth, Virginia

After the Siege of Suffolk, the 16th Conn. moved on to Portsmouth, Virginia, near the Elizabeth River. The camp was a wonderful site, giving the men time to bathe and enjoy sailing and fishing. Time here was short, and they were ordered on the March again to Yorktown and Whitehouse Landing. It was here that General Dix arrived and the Dix's Peninsula Campaign in Virginia began. From late June to early July, the Regiment marched, through the hottest of conditions. Men fell out and died from heat stroke. The Confederates pursued the Union Army, forcing hard marching to stay ahead of the enemy. All along the path of this march were luscious, large blackberries, prompting the campaign to be named the 'Blackberry Raid.'

At the conclusion of Dix's Campaign, the regiment returned to Portsmouth, Virginia where they remained for many months. Gradually, they made camp their home. As a result of a special order, the 16th Conn. formed a band, which grew the stature of the regiment. Lyman B. Wilcox is assumed to have been a member of this band.

July 18, 1863
Camp of 16th Conn. Vols., Portsmouth, Va.

My very dear Brother Robbie
I received your very welcome letter last night but I was astonished to think that you had not heard from me, for I have written half a dozen letters to you within a few days. However I think you will have received them before this as your letter was dated the 10th. But in case you had not rec'd any of them, I will write this and relieve your minds as you desired me to. I was not hurt or did not receive any injury in our last campaign, only I got pretty well tired out. How is the draft progressing up in old

Connecticut. We are hearing great stories about it down here. One story is that there was a great riot in Hartford and that there were 3 men killed and that the draft had been suspended by order of the Governor. Whether there is any truth or not to any of these stories I do not know. But I presume that there is not. But they have been having a great time in New York *[New York Draft Riots]* have they not. All of the papers that we get are full of it.

I think that it is a shame for them to act so. They had ought to have a Brigade of Soldiers there and force them to come down here at the point of the Bayonet. It was all very nice as long as they could sit in their easy chairs at home and read their papers and say why don't the army do this and do that but as soon as they are asked to come down here and help, Oh! There is where it makes them howl.

A man that refuses to come down here when they are drafted to come ought to be shot down like a dog for he is not fit to live.

It is all very nice for them to stay at home. But I rather think the day will soon come when they will have to live under canvass also.

I expect that our Reg. will have to be filled up with conscripts as well as the rest. Though "the Lord knows" that the Reg. is bad enough without any of <u>those</u> in it.

If there is anything that is despised out here it is a Reg. of conscripts for they were never known to stand fire and their share of the work generally has to fall on the Vol's.

There has been 3 Commissioned Officers and 6 non-commissioned officers appointed out of this Reg. to proceed to Conn. and suprentend the enrolling of conscripts for this Reg. We require about 500 men to fill our maximum number. **Corp. Moses McCrum** of Co. G is one of the non-coms appointed to go to Conn. I should like to go on that business very well but I believe there is no musicians required. Having nothing more to say I think I will close. Please write soon and please ask Aunt Hattie if she won't write to me when she finds nothing more important to do. With much love I remain ever

Your Aff Brother

Lyman B. Wilcox

P.S. Please ask Grandma to send me a few postage stamps if she
can share them as this one is the last that I have.
L.B.W.

Grave of Moses McCrum in Wilcox Cemetery, East Berlin, CT

McCrum, *Moses; Sergeant, Company G; Residence, Berlin,
Connecticut; Enlisted August 8, 1862; Mustered August 24, 1862;
Captured at Plymouth, NC, April 20, 1864; Died in prison, Charleston,
SC, October 2, 1864.*

Summer in Portsmouth, Virginia

July 20, 1863
Camp of 16th Conn. Vols., Portsmouth, Va.

My very dear Robbie,

I rec'd your very welcome letter and papers last night and very glad I was to get them.

You wish to know what I think about your enlisting in the 3 months service. My advice would be to keep out of the service altogether, or at least for the present. Take my word for it. If you live two years longer you will see all of the soldiering that you want to. Therefore keep out of it while you can. And then there is another thing. If ever you do enlist try to get a little higher situation than a drummer. For while a drummer you do not stand any chance for promotion. As a private you would have a sight of being promoted to Corporal and from that to a Sergeant. After that your promotion would be quite rapid provided you behaved yourself. I think Robbie that you had better <u>play</u> soldier for a little while longer though what service you would see in the state never would hurt you, neither would it give you any idea of a soldier's life. If you are agoing to try to be a good drummer you will find it is the hardest work that you ever tried. You can have no idea of it until you try it, and I would advise you not to do that. But I must close now as I have got a big washing to do today. Please write soon and often. Give my love to all the dear folks and occasionally remember while you are enjoying yourself. Your Aff Brother, down in Dixie.
Lyman B. Wilcox

July 23, 1863
Camp of 16th Conn. Vols., Portsmouth, Va.

My very dear Robbie,

I rec'd your last letter yesterday and you may rest assured that I am not "sick of your nonsense" yet as you was pleased to call it. In fact you cannot write too often to suit me.

Field Music: From Antietam to Andersonville

Enclosed you will find a piece of <u>that</u> <u>tree</u> that you wanted. It is a piece that I brought from Yorktown in my pocket book, and though not quite so good a piece as that was that I sent you before, still it is the best that I can obtain. You also wished to know what I preferred in the reading line. Well I am not very particular as long as it is something to busy myself with. If you could without any inconvenience I think some such paper as the "Flag of our Union", "Your Flag", or a "Waverly" occasionally would be perhaps the cheapest that you could send, and at the same time they would be very acceptable. As for the cost I will make that all right and more too, if we are ever paid off again. I suppose that you do not have any more pocket money than you know how to use. But as I said, when we get paid off I will send you all that I can. Moses McCrum left here this morning for Conn. You will have a good chance to see him I think if you wish to. He is going to help bring on the conscripts.

I had some things that I meant to send home by him, but I did not on account of leaving rather unexpectedly. I wish that you could come down here and make me a visit. I think that we could have a splendid time. There is only three in my tent and there is plenty of room for as many more. What a glorious old time we could have. But I suppose that there is no use in thinking of it, for it is an impossibility. You say that you have given up all idea of enlisting as you think you are too young. I am very glad that you have come to that conclusion, for it is just what I thought myself. If you ever want to serve Uncle Sam, don't try the army, but go into the navy, that is the place. I think I shall try it if I ever get out of the army. Not that I am sick of the army by any means, only that it is such a lasy life.

I have just received the "Hartford Post" that you sent me, and I am very much obliged to you for it. I have just finished reading it having read it through, advertisements and all, and now feel as if I should like to read it through again. You cannot imagine how much we prize reading that we receive from home. Have they drafted in New Britain yet. If they have, please let me know if there is any body that I know and those from Berlin too. I

60

suppose that I shall have a chance to see some of them before long. We are having very good times here now, only it is almost too easy. We are <u>living</u> in clover too, for we have some two or three large secesh *[secession]* farms to forage off from. I went out yesterday evening on a little raid all by myself and succeeded in bringing in enough provisions to last me some time. The forage consists of Potatoes, cabbages, cucumbers, tomatoes and Peaches, generally, and you may bet high that all of those articles are well represented in my tent.

There ---- I declare. I have just rec'd another letter bearing your well known hand writing and the date of July 21st, and I think that I will answer it all in this one, though it will prevent me sending you that large envelope of curiosities. But I will send it Robbie as soon as I can obtain postage stamps. And now for the letter. Those Black-berries you will have to see before you can form any idea of them. I will not try to tell you about them for you will think that I am stretching the story considerably, but Rob if I can ever have a chance I will take you down here and let you see them yourself. As for the "Soldier's Life" I am all right on that. I like it a great deal better than I did when I first came out here. For now I have got so used to it that it seems almost as if I had been one all my life. I do not care about coming home on a furlough until I see this war all settled up right. I should like to see you all very much indeed, but I shall not try to until I can come home for good. Now I think that I must bid you good bye, for my letter is getting a great deal longer than I meant to have it. Please write soon and often and give my love to Uncle Lester, Aunt Hattie and the children. And reserve a good share for yourself.

  With much love I remain,

  Your aff Soldier Brother,

   Lyman B. Wilcox

  I will send you those things as soon as I can.

   Yours,

   Lyman B.

August 5, 1863
Camp of 16th Conn. Vols., Portsmouth, Va.

My very dear Robbie,
    I have just received your very welcome letter and the paper that you sent me. I am very much obliged to you for sending me the papers and I take a great deal of pleasure in reading them. I have to lend them nearly all over the Reg. after I have finished reading them.
    Robbie we are just about to be paid off. We signed the payrolls night before last, for 2 months pay and are expecting to be paid tomorrow. I shall send home all that I can spare, but I am afraid that it will not be much.
    We are still at our old camp near the sea shore and we have got things fixed up very comfortable. We have got shade trees set out all around our tents and inside we have nice bunks and beds filled with corn husks in the place of straw. We have also got tables, a brick floor, and a cellar just large enough to keep our bread, and such things in.
    Last Sunday we had an alarm, and I thought that we had got to march sure. I was at the time very pleasantly established under a shade tree reading those papers that Aunt Hattie sent me, when the orders came to be ready to march immediately with 3 days rations. Well in an instant every one was flying around and packing up as quick as possible. I packed my "haversack" and filled my canteen, rolled my half-tent and rubber blanket and was then ready to go. But this time we were in luck, for just as we were ready, the orders were countermanded, so all that we had to do was to unpack and make up our beds again.
    "Every thing is lovely" down here and "the goose hangs high".
        With much love I remain
            Your Aff. Brother,
            Lyman B. Wilcox
P.S. Please write soon and often, and remember how welcome those papers are. I will make it all right when we are paid. I will

send you those things for your museum when I can find anything worth sending.

Aug. 11, 1863
Camp of 16th Conn. Vols., Portsmouth, Va.

My very dear Robbie,

I have just rec'd your very welcome letter and it pleased me so much that I am determined to answer it at once. I think that it is rather strange that you have not rec'd my letters as I have wrote you two or three lately. You was never more mistaken if you thought that I was mad with you. If you don't hear from me very often I don't want to have you feel worried about me. For I shall write as often as I can. I am very sorry that you feel lonesome where you are. But I hope that you will get over that feeling as soon as possible. Who is that Willie Atwood that you spoke about in your letter, is he the fellow that used to go around with Jim Lamb or the one that was clerk in Riley's store. The fact is that I have been out here so long and made so many new acquaintances that I have almost forgotten those that I used to know.

I am very glad to know that you are agoing to send me on those things by Willie Atwood and I will take the first opportunity to run over and see if he has come. You say that you want to write to Samuel. He is Company I, 15th Conn. Vol's.

I wish if you could find it out that you would send me on Charlie Brandegee's address when you write to me again.

That was quite a "Tradegy" about Frank and Wm. Booth. Quite a battle in fact and I suppose Frank thinks that there was some great flank movement come over him & I think that he was glad to change his base of operations.

I suppose Robbie that you would like to know how I am getting along about now. Well I am getting on first rate considering the warmth of the weather. Robbie if you want to know what real hot weather is you will have to come down here to find it. We don't have to work any at all now on account of the weather being so hot that they are afraid of the men getting sun-struck. So all that we have to do is to lie still in the coolest place that one can find and even then we cannot begin to keep cool. I can hardly remember when I have had a dry rag of clothes on my back I sweat so much. We go to bed at night with clothes wet through and wake up in the morning with them even wetter were it possible. You may think that I am making a big story about it, but it is true every word of it.

I wrote a letter to Aunt Hattie this afternoon and just after closing it I received yours which I am trying to answer now. I am seated in my tent at the table with my drum for a seat while **Bryant** my bed fellow is lying on the bunk by my side reading by the same light. Bryant is one of the best fellows in the corps, and he is only about a year older than you are. He is the youngest in the "Drum Corps". He is in Co. I. My watch is hanging on the tent pole close by my head and it says 10 min. to 8. and there goes the drum for Tattoo so I must get ready to go out and drum. After that we will have to go to bed so I think that I will bid you Good night my very dear Brother Robbie. I wish that I was near enough to say Good night to you. But I fear that it will be some time before I have the pleasure.

Civil War Volunteer Infantry drummers in a casual pose

I get so mad sometimes that I almost think that I never <u>will</u> go home if I cannot go pretty soon. But I suppose that when the time does come if nothing happens we shall enjoy ourselves much. Give my love and respects to all the dear folks and remember me occasionally as

       Your Aff. Brother,
          Lyman B. Wilcox

Bryant, George H.; Musician, Company I; Residence, Hartford, Connecticut; Enlisted July 16, 1862; Mustered August 24, 1862; Captured at Plymouth, NC, April 20, 1864; Died in prison, Charleston, SC, September 25, 1864.

August 13, 1863
Camp of 16th Conn. Vols., Portsmouth, Va

My very dear Robbie,

I have rec'd your letter of the 10th to day and as you seem to take it so hard because I have not written to you, I think I must send you something to reconcile you. Therefore I send you by this mail a "Soldiers Memorial" of Co. G" which I think you would like to look at.

I have sent you quite a number of letters lately and I think that it is very strange that you have not rec'd them. About sending me anything by Moses McCrum, you can send me just what you are a mind to. Those things that you said you was agoing to send would be very acceptable, especially the cigars and a little Killicinick Tobacco would not go bad. But send what you are a mind to. Give my love to the dear folks at home and please write often.

    In haste, Rob with much love I remain,
        Your Aff Brother
        Lyman B. Wilcox

Field Music: From Antietam to Andersonville

August 17, 1863
Camp of 16ᵗʰ Conn. Vols., Portsmouth, VA

My very dear Robbie,

Having spare time just at present I thought I would write you a few lines. I think that I am likely to have plenty of spare time now for quite a little while, for this morning when I went to take my usual morning bath in the river I cut my foot with a piece of shell so that I can hardly stir. It is nothing very serious I think but it is very painful and will lay me up for more that a fortnight. I have just had it dressed and it feels so much easier that I thought I would write to you as you have complained so much lately about not receiving more letter from me. I rec'd a paper bearing your well known hand writing yesterday for which I am very much obliged to you indeed. Robbie I am agoing to get my "bounty check" next week and then I will send you a dollar or two. I would have sent you some out of my pay but you know that I wanted to send Grandma all that I could.

I am agoing to get you some cotton flowers for your museum if you want them. I think that a little of "King Cotton" would look well at the head of your collection. There is about an acre of the article not a great ways from our camp and I would have sent the blossoms in this letter if I could possibly walk down in the field.

Saml. O. was over here just now and I told him that you said that you meant to write to him and he said that he should like to have you very much. There comes the mail now and I'll bet $10 that I will have a letter from you. Yes sure enough so there is and a book too. "Bully for Rob".

But "for me", Rob, I think you must have been drunk when you wrote it, or was it that soda water that you drank with Jim Whaples. I hope that you wont 'spree it' too much now that Uncle Lester is gone. Give my best respects to that Jim Whaples that you spoke about in your letter. I think that I must have known him once, at least the name sounds familiar. What kind of a fellow is he, is he the same old "Whape" that he used to be. If he is just drink another glass of soda water with him for me, and charge it to the Quarter-Master of the 16th C.V. (Cold Victuals.)

But I must close now as my foot begins to ache again. Write soon and often. Give my love and respects to all my friends in New Britain.

Your most Aff Soldier Brother,
Lyman B. Wilcox

Saml. O. is here now and he says direct his letters to
Saml O. Fowler
Co. I. 15th Conn. Vols,
Portsmouth,
VA

We have just had news that "Sumpter" is taken. Would to God that it was true.

Fowler, Samuel O.; Private, 15th Connecticut Infantry Regiment, Company I; Residence, Branford, Connecticut; Enlisted August 12, 1862; Mustered August 25, 1862; Mustered out June 27, 1865.

August 19, 1863
Camp of 16th Conn. Vols., Portsmouth, Va

My very dear Robbie,

I send you enclosed in this letter $1.00. I wish that I could send you more but I cannot possibly this time though I hope to soon. I hope that it will make it all right for what you have sent me. I will send you more as soon as possible. Please drink a glass of soda water out of it for me.

I must close now. Please write soon and remember,
Your Aff Brother,
Lyman B. Wilcox

P.S. If you send me anything by Moses McCrum, will you please put in a few leather shoe strings (a thing which it is impossible to buy down here) and one or two pieces of waxed ends if it will not be too much trouble.

>Yours,
>
>Lyman B.

August 28, 1863
Camp of 16th Conn. Vols., Portsmouth, Va

My dear brother Robbie
    I have just received your very welcome letter of the 21st and very glad I was to hear from you. I have just received a letter from Charlie Brandegee. He was in camp at Beverly Ford when he wrote to me. This is the second letter that I have had from him since I have been out.
    I am glad to hear that you received that Memorial safe. I had begun to think that you had not received it. **Sergeant Kimball** was reduced for staying away from the Reg. so long. He has been in the New Haven Hospital ever since the battle of Antietam. **Charlie Roys** was slightly wounded in the leg, but only just enough to get his name on the list. So you have really seen Tom Thumb have you, well that is something that I have not seen. But I think that I am ahead of you on the sight seeing question. I have seen what I hope you never will have a chance to see.
    Enclosed you will find that cotton blossom that I promised to send you. But you cannot tell anything how it looks by it. When I first picked it it was white, after I had pressed it for a little while, it was yellow and then it turned red and now it is Blackish purple. What color it will be when you get it I cannot say. Yesterday we moved our camp about six miles and are now no longer near the salt water. Our Reg. has got charge of a Fort Griswold and are now very busy repairing it. To day it is raining all of the while. It is a steady, cold, disagreeable rain and this forenoon as of course it was to wet to practice on our drums so I rolled myself in my

blanket and curled myself up on my bunk and read some old New York Ledgers. But I soon read those through and then what the deuce to do I did not know so I commenced drumming on our table just to busy myself with. But my fun soon stopped there for the first thing I knew out dropped the leg of our table. Then I had a job to mend that and I had just got it done and was wondering what I should do next when your "bully" letter came and some papers to which I suppose came from Aunt Hattie as you said nothing about them in your letter. If so please thank her very much for me. But I must close now and go down to the cook's tent and draw my supper which consists of Bread and Coffee as usual. Please excuse the poor writing as my table is rather rickety yet.

> With much love I remain
> Your Aff. Brother
> Lyman B. Wilcox

John P. Stannard from New Britain, our Drum Sergeant has been appointed Drum Major of this Reg.

Kimball, George; Sergeant, Company G; Residence, Hartford, Connecticut; Enlisted July 29, 1862; Reduced in rank to Private due to sickness on March 6, 1863; Transferred to Co. F, Reserve troops on July 20, 1863; Mustered out July 6, 1865.

Roys, Charles A.; Sergeant, Company G; Residence, Berlin, Connecticut; Enlisted August 7, 1862; Discharged June 16, 1865.

Stannard, John P.; Principal Musician, Field & Staff; Residence, Farmington, Connecticut; Enlisted July 22, 1862; Mustered August 24, 1862; Captured at Plymouth, NC, April 20, 1864; Paroled November 30, 1864; Mustered out June 24, 1865.

Chapter 5
Autumn in Portsmouth, Virginia

The 16th Conn. Regiment remained in Portsmouth through the autumn months. The men took pride in their encampment, with neat order prevailing. As the winter months approached, the men built a log hospital, log houses for the officers, log kitchens, as well as eating lodges for all the men. Additionally, a chapel was raised. The men were getting a much needed rest from the travails of war.

The following letter is from Samuel O. Fowler, cousin of Lyman B. and Robert M. Wilcox, addressed to Robert at the home of L.L. Booth in New Britain, Connecticut.

September 5, 1863
Camp near Portsmouth [*Virginia*]

Dear Cousin Robert
        I received your letter duly, and was very glad to receive a letter from you. Saw Lyman a few days after he cut his foot he said he was doing well. I have seen him once since, and he was getting along "right smart" then, and think he is doing well at this time. Ever since I received your letter I have tried to go and see him but cannot without a pass signed by Gen. Giddy, and none are granted at this time. We are all at work on defences forts and rifle pits – nine hours per day. Besides our own regiment, there are nearly a regiment of Negroes at work with shovels all of the time. In regarding to the life of a soldier I would say that I get along very well and am willing to stay out my time of enlistment and am not sorry I am in the army. The cause in which we are engaged is well worth the sacrifices that we are making, well worth all the trials and all the difficulties that beset our path. Well Robbie set down now with me and take your maps and see just where Lyman and myself and our whole brigade marched a short

time ago when we went on what everyone calls the "blackberry raid" where nobody was hurt and no harm to any of us done. We were encamping a short distance from our present camping ground. We are now about 6 miles south of the city of Portsmouth and the 16th where Lyman is, about one mile north of us encamped in a dry place near a cornfield. We are now encamped on the west branch of the Elisabeth river. The first of June we marched to Portsmouth and went aboard a steamer and sailed up to as far as Yorktown and stopped two or three days and we went claming – round ones very nice ones too. Leaving this place we steamed up as far as whitehouse. This was the terminus of our journey in a steamer. We now commenced our weary march of over one hundred miles through a country of beauty. The fields were rich with waving grain of a golden hue, ready for the reaper. On we passed some, yes, a large number, falling out by the road side, wearied exhausted by marching and the intense heat. On the third of July we encamped on a wheat field of one hundred acres belonging to a man by the name Henry Taylor a strong secessionist. He had one son in the rebel army and owned before the war broke out seven hundred slaves but now he has less than half that number. "Sept 7" My time has been taken up most of the time since writing the above till now. We spent our fourth of July in the wheat field and about 12 o'clock that night we heard the large guns about 12 miles distant for some two hours. The next day we moved from the wheat field encamping near there on a high hill and here and in the fields near us we could pick as many blackberries as we wanted so it was our own fault if we went without. Hundreds of bushels were picked on the 5th of July. The next day we had orders to return on our homeward march.

I have been thinking for some time that I would like to have you send a likeness of yourself of those small ??? ones, and if you will I pay you for one. I suppose Lyman has given all of the news contained in my letter before now. I would like to hear from you often – write as often as convenient.

Yours truly

Samuel O. Fowler

Lyman B. also continued his correspondence.

September 11, 1863
Camp of 16th Conn. Vols., Portsmouth, VA

My very dear Brother Robbie,
      It has been some time since I have heard from you, and thinking perhaps you did not receive that last letter that I wrote to you, so I will try you again. I wrote you in my last letter that a part of the Regt. had gone to South Carolina. They have not returned yet, and they will probably stay there some time. We have been boarding up our tents this week as the nights are getting to be so cold that the cold air came through the tents. But we have not as yet rec'd any orders to prepare for winter quarters. I hope that we shall soon. How would you like to come down here and make me a visit of a week or two if we stay here this winter. I have got a "Bully" good bunk just wide enough for two, and a plenty of thick woolen blankets, so that I guess that we could make you comfortable without much trouble. But I am afraid that it will be so that you cannot come. We would have a first rate time though if you did. How are you getting along in N.B. *[New Britain]* now, and are you going to school yet. I hope that you will not miss any opportunity that you may have of going to school this winter. Does Hattie go to school now, and how is she getting along. I have not heard from her for a long while.
      Robbie what have you done with all the things that I left you when I enlisted. My Books, Papers, Drawing Instruments & Pencils and all the other trash that I left lying around the shop and house.
      I do not care anything about them and you can do what you choose with them, as I suppose you have done long ago. And Robbie is there any Pigeons left on the old place or have they all deserted. I suppose of course now that there is nobody to take care of them that they have left for better quarters.
      Mr. Bryon Atwater arrived here yesterday and brought me a package from Grandma. He offered to take home anything that I

may want to send, but Rob I cannot for the life of me find anything that I can send to you. If I could only get a pass to the city of Portsmouth I could find something worth sending to you, but as it is I cannot. I hope you will forgive me but I would get you something if I possibly could.

But I must stop now. We have an inspection and review this afternoon and I must begin to get ready. I am in first rate health now and I hope this may find you the same. Love to all. With much love I remain,

> Your Aff. Brother
> Lyman B. Wilcox

September 27, 1863
Camp of 16th Conn. Vols., Portsmouth, Va

My very dear Brother,

I hope you will forgive me for not writing to you before this but the fact is Robbie I have been rather sick for a week or two back and since I have got well I have not been able to get any postage stamps before this evening. I was taken with the Diptheria the evening after attending the funeral of **Saml. Woodruff**.

My throat was so that I could hardly breathe at one time but thank God it never got any worse than that. I used to have to get it burned out every morning and through the day I had to gargle "nitrate of silver" and something else composed of iron and zinc that was strong enough to burn my neck through almost. But I am entirely well now and I think that I shall take pretty good care and not get the Diptheria again if I can help it.

But I must close now in order to send this by the mail and I suppose that you want to hear from me as soon as possible. I will write again soon. Give my love to all and reserve a good share for yourself.

> Your Aff. Brother.
> Lyman B. Wilcox

I suppose you think this is short and not very sweet but I will write again soon.

       Yours,

          Lyman

Woodruff, Samuel E.; Sergeant, Company G; Residence, Berlin, Connecticut; Enlisted July 25, 1862; Mustered August 24, 1862; Died of diphtheria September 17, 1863.

Grave of Samuel Woodruff in Maple Cemetery, Berlin, Connecticut

October 1, 1863
Camp of 16th Conn. Vols., Portsmouth, Va.

My very dear Brother Robbie,

      Once more I have an opportunity to write to you and as I suppose that you are always glad to hear from me I will try to tell you all how we are situated here. We have got a first rate camp now. We are situated about 2 miles and a half from the city of Portsmouth and we are only a few steps from the Headquarters of Gen. G. W. Getty who formerly commanded our Division (the 3rd) but now commands this Department. He is a regular old 'war dog' and is a great favorite of all the boys here. Our camp is on a branch of the Elizabeth river called Deep Creek and that you may know how a camp is laid out I will send you a 'ground plan' of ours. You will see where I have marked out my tent. We drummers have a whole street to ourselves. There is not but two in my tent now, one besides myself, and for the last day or two we have been boarding up the tent and making a new bunk (we both sleep together now) and we have got lots of room and are as comfortable as you can imagine. I would not exchange with you as good a bed as you have got. Tomorrow or next day we expect a stove, we have sent to Baltimore for one and then we shall be all right for the winter. How I wish that you could come on here and stay with me a little while. I know you would enjoy it very much, and Bryant, my tent and mess mate says that he should like to see you very much. He is not much older than you are and he is a "Bully" fellow.

Annexed I send you a small diagram of my tent as it is now. It is built up of boards as high as your head and then the tent is set on top of that so you see that we have abundance of room. Our bunks are made just high enough so that we can set our drums under it and so you see that they are not in the way any at all. And Robbie I have got one of the prettiest little puppies that you ever saw. He is jet black and his coat shines like a dollar.

If you were fortunate enough to come on here I think we could make you comfortable while you staid. We have got a first rate bed made of corn husks and the bunk is a plenty wide enough for three and then we have four good thick woolen blankets so I guess cold would not trouble you.

But I must close now Robbie as it is time for Tattoo or bed time so Good Bye.

Your Aff Brother
Lyman B. Wilcox

Love to all and reserve a good share for yourself.
L.

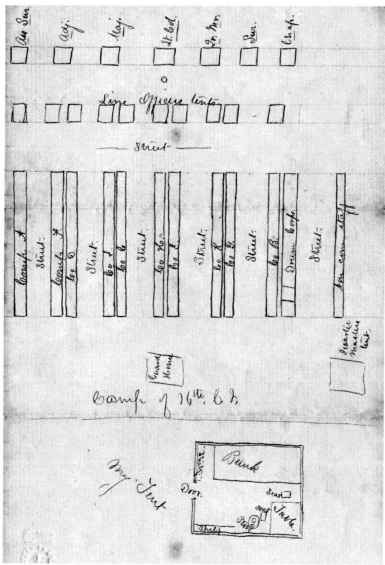

Lyman B.'s diagram of his tent and camp

Autumn in Portsmouth, Virginia

October 11, 1863
Camp of 16th Conn. Vols., Portsmouth, Va.

My dear Brother Robbie

I have just rec'd your very welcome letter and as you was so kind to write me such a long letter I think that I must answer it at once. But I shall be pretty careful and not write you another such a letter as I did before. I did not think when I wrote it that it would make you so crazy to come out here. If I had I should not have written it.

You must keep in mind that what I have written is only the bright side of the subject. If you should only see the other side. I fancy a soldiers life would not look so facinating not even if shared in my company which you seem I think so much of.

But I shall not tell you anything about the dark side of the picture now. You had better give up all idea of coming out here to stay for it never would suit you as well as it does me. You will never find a place where you will enjoy yourself as well as you do where you are now. And if you leave it I am sure that you will regret it all of your life. You had better do the best that you can where you are and you can rest assured that you will lose nothing by doing your duty faithfully. I have had that knocked into me since I have been out here and I have never known it to fail.

I should very much like to have you make me a visit out here. But Rob I shall never help you to come out here to stay so I think that the best thing that you can do is to give up the idea.

What business is Mr. Isacc Stanley in now and what is By Chamberlain doing. I believe that he was in the bank when I left was they not. If you see them I wish that you would give them my best respects. What is Willie Parsons doing now. The same as usual? I believe you said in one of your letters that he was Drummer for the New Britain Company did you not. I should like an opportunity of drumming with him for a little while. I used to think that he was about as good a drummer as I had ever seen.

But I must close now Robbie so Good bye for the present. Give my love and best respects to Uncle Lester, Aunt Hattie and the rest and reserve a good share for yourself. Please write soon and often and remember me as

Your Aff Brother

Lyman B. Wilcox

October 18, 1863
Camp of 16th Conn. Vols., Portsmouth, Va.

My very dear Grandma,

I wrote you some days ago about some clothing for winter and if you conclude to send them (which I hope you will) I wish that you would put in addition some butter, tea & sugar if you can without inconvenience. And I should also like a small earthen plate, tea cup & saucer and a tea-spoon if you can just put them in. And what ever else you are a mind to put in. Whatever it is, it shall not be any expense to you for I will try to send home enough next pay day to make it all right.

I hardly think that I shall need anything in the shape of gloves or mittens as it is impossible to drum with them on.

But some of Aunt Polly's stockings would not be a bad thing.

But I must close now. Please give my love to Aunt Mary, Hattie, Aunt Polly & the rest and write to me soon. With much love I remain,

Your Aff. Grandson

Lyman B. Wilcox

P.S. The box if you send it by express should be directed to
Co. G. 16th Conn. Vol's.
Portsmouth Va.
Instead of to Washington as the letters are.

Autumn in Portsmouth, Virginia

October 19, 1863
Camp of 16th Conn. Vols., Portsmouth, Va.

My very dear Robbie,
    I have just rec'd your very welcome letter and as you wished me to answer at once I have accordingly set about it. I am very glad that you have changed your mind about coming down here to stay and I am sure that you will never regret it. I intend to keep up good spirits while I remain in "Unculpsalms" service and if I do not I do not intend that you shall ever know it, or any one else. That's my style. I should be very happy indeed to see that picture that you mentioned and if you obtain it send it along & I will return it to you if you wish it. Lieut. Andrus left here for Conn. about a week ago and I hope that you will succeed in seeing him for those things that you spoke about would be very acceptable indeed, just the things that I wanted. I will agree to that bargain that you wished to make with me provided that I always have the postage stamps to carry it out. That is what bothers me the most.
    I hear from Charlie Brandegee quite often. When I last heard from him he was encamped at Beverly Ford, VA, and had just been promoted from camp clerk to Adjutant clerk. A first rate berth. I will enclose you his last letter that you may read it yourself. But I must close now as it is about noon and I have just heard the cry of "Co. G. fall in for your Roast Beef", so here goes. Enclosed I send a note to Grandma and I wish that you would carry it to her if you happen to be going down there next Sunday. Please give my respects Cousins and the other boys and tell them that I should be delighted to hear from them. Give my love and best respects to Uncle Lester & Aunt Hattie & the rest. With much love I remain,
      Your Aff Brother,
        Lyman B. Wilcox

Following is the above referenced letter from Charlie Brandegee to Lyman B. Wilcox, dated October 5th, 1863, from a camp near Culpepper, Virginia:

Dear Friend,

It is high time you last kind letter was answered. But you must bear in mind that I have been exceedingly busy for the past week making out the monthly returns, reports + etc. I am glad to hear you are still in good health. I heard via Comet that you were attacked by the disease that is prevailing in your department. I also heard of the death of our fellow townsman Samuel Woodruff. "Sic itur ad astra". *[Thus one goes to the stars.]* Our schoolmates are passing away one by one. I look back and recall the changes of the past two years & I can hardly realize that 24 months would alter every thing so much. But so it is. Nothing of interest to note here. I do not imagine that we will trouble Richmond much this fall. All the work is going to be done out west. Two corps of this army have gone to reinforce Roscrans *[Gen. Rosecrans]* & another is rumored to be going. There was some firing out in front yesterday.

But I must think of stopping. Success to you and to all the representatives of "Old Berlin". May they never grow less is the prayer of your's.

Very Respectfully

October 24, 1863
Camp of 16th Conn. Vols., Portsmouth, Va.

My very dear Brother,

I received your letter the other day but I am sorry to say that I must "dash your new born hopes to the ground" so soon. You seemed quite confident of seeing me very soon but Rob the fact is I have not applied for a furlough yet as the captain says that the men that have families must go home first and there will not be the least shadow of a chance of my obtaining one until spring if

I do then. So you see that you will have to give up seeing me for a while yet. Night before last we received orders to march immediately with 10 days rations but the orders were countermanded before we started. Many thanks for that. I expect that if we had started we should have gone up the Peninsular way again. And it would be nothing strange if we went now. I am rather sorry that you concluded <u>not</u> to send on those things by Lieut. Andrews but I suppose that it will do just as well to have them come in the box if Grandma will send it. I have not heard from her for a long while. There was a Dr. Wright hung here today for shooting **Lieut. Sanborn** of one of the colored Reg'ts stationed here some time ago. I think you will remember it as it was in all the papers at the time. Well night before last when he was confined in the Portsmouth jail his daughter (a young lady of about 20 years) obtained permission to visit him for a little while, and while there, managed by some means to exchange clothes with the old gentleman so you see that when the time expired the old fellow just walks out and nobody knows the odds until all the guards are passed except the last one and there the Lieut. of the Guards happens to be at the time who remarks as the supposed young lady walks past him that she appears to have grown taller since she went in a few hours ago and smelling a rather large mice he nabs her and sure enough it was the old Gentleman himself who quietly walks back into his commodious quarters again. There was a carriage and Horses awaiting him just beyond our pickets but they did not carry the old "chappie" off that time and now he has gone to that bourne from which such old cusses never return. *Thank God!*

But I must close now so adieu. Wife and Family are all well and send love.

Yours most Aff
Lyman B. Wilcox

To Mr. Robert M. Wilcox, Chief Executive Clerk of the Retail Boot & Shoe Warehouse of L.L. Booth,
New Britain, Connecticut

Sanborn, *Alanson L., of Thetford, VT, 1st Lieutenant, USCI, on July 11, 1863, while drilling his soldiers in Norfolk, VA, was murdered by Dr. D. M. Wright, who was promptly hung for committing this outrage. Lt. Sanborn entered the volunteer service from a pure sense of duty, and it is said that he believed he would never return home; he was willing to give his life for his country and for freedom, and died a martyr's death.*

Vermonters who served as Officers in the United States Colored Troops
©1996-2006, VermontCivilWar.Org

October 30, 1863
Camp of 16th Conn. Vols., Portsmouth, Va.

My very dear Brother Robbie,
I rec'd your letter of the 26th inst. this noon and as I have nothing else to do this afternoon I will write you a [few] lines. I am very sorry indeed to hear that you have the sore throat and I hope that you will take good care that it does not get any worse. Henry Savage got back here the day before yesterday and brought a small bundle for me from home containing among other things some chocolate and a Book from Robbie which I prize very much. I am sure Rob that I can never half thank you sufficiently for the great kindness that you show me. But I am in hopes some day to be able to express my thanks in something more substantially than mere words. I had a letter from you a week or two ago about my getting a furlough and you say "<u>now you will not want to desert.</u>"
Now Robbie that is coming back on me with a vengeance. Just as if I ever thought of deserting. Well you must have a poor idea of my patriotism if you think that I entertain any such idea. No-Sir'ee. I shall stay here until my time is up or I receive an <u>Honorable</u> discharge. And that I do not want yet awhile. You must not think that every body is as discontented as you are. It is only a little over twenty one months that I have got to stay out

82

here and that will soon pass away if I have good news from home often.

Sat. Oct 31st – I am sorry Robbie that I could not finish my letter yesterday, but just as I got into the middle of it Sam Fowler came over here and as I had not seen him for about 2 months I had to stop and talk with him and when he left it was so dark that I had to put it off until today. Sam says that he rec'd a letter from you and he thought that he should have to answer it at once. He sends his respects to you and all of his acquaintances up that way. Last Sunday I had a visit from **Willie Atwood** and we had a first rate time. He gave me an account of nearly every thing that has happened since I left and all about New Britain in general.

I have just received yours of the 30th and am very sorry that you was so dissappointed. But you cannot feel any worse about it that I do. But never mind Rob. It will be only 21 months before I shall be home for good. To be sure you will be a little older then than you are now but that will not prevent us enjoying ourselves will it. But I must say good bye now for a day or two. Give my love & respects to all at home. With much love I remain,

Your Aff. Brother
Lyman B. Wilcox

Atwood, William A.; Private, 15th Connecticut Infantry Regiment, Company F; Residence, Berlin, Connecticut; Enlisted August 25, 1862; Mustered out June 27, 1865.

November 6, 1863
Camp of 16th Conn. Vols., Portsmouth, Va.

My very dear Robbie

Having spare time this evening I thought that perhaps you would like to hear from me. I have just come in from a two hour drill. As Drummer of the Guard I had to Drum for the Reg. while on Battalion drill and I tell you what Robbie it is any thing but fun when you make a business of it. A Drum is a very pretty thing to play with but when you have to earn your living by Drumming it is not quite so much fun.

Union Field Musicians, including drummers like Lyman B. Wilcox

Tomorrow I shall probably see something that I have not seen before – the execution of 2 men from the 8th Conn. for desertion. They are to be shot at 10 o'clock and if I witness it, I will write you an account of the affair. Our Reg. has had orders to attend, and of course they will not go without the "Drum Corps." I rec'd a letter from Charlie Brandegee yesterday dated at Warrenton Junction saying that he was well etc. Warrenton Junction is a place that we marched through last fall on our march from Harpers Ferry to Fredericksburg under Burnside. It was a tough old place when we came through there and at one of the camps – which even to this day goes by the name of "Starvation Hollow", - we went five days without having any rations dealt out to us and three out of the five without anything to eat except what corn we could steal from the mules. Those were rough old times. But we have got soup for supper and as I am pretty hungry I think that I must bid you <u>Au</u> <u>Revoir</u>.

>With much love I remain
>Your Aff Brother
>Lyman B. Wilcox

P.S. For want of something better I will drink the very good health of your Grammar School beauty in a cup of coffee.

>Here is to her &c &c
>Yours
>L.B.W.

November 7, 1863
Camp of 16th Conn. Vols., Portsmouth, Va.

My very dear Robbie,
I Rec'd your letter of the 3rd this noon and very glad indeed was I to hear from you. I thank you a thousand times for getting me those books and I am very glad to hear that you think so much of me. Robbie you do not know how much good it did me to hear that you had concluded to settle down to a trade, and I think you have chosen a first rate one, one that will suit you and I hope that you will prosper in it. Who do you think you shall learn your trade of or have not you made up your mind yet. I hope that you will stick to your trade now you have chosen it and I will do all that I can to help you. You say that you are agoing to school this winter well. I hope you will learn all that you can for it will probably be the last chance that you will ever have to go to school. In my last letter I promised to tell you about the execution of those men in the 8th Conn. Well Friday morning we were all ready and had our Guard Mounting an hour & a half sooner on purpose to attend the "Shouting Match" as some of our Boys termed it and were about half way to the ground (which is 3 miles from our

camp) when an orderly rode up and informed us that the ceremonies were post-poned until Monday the 9th so we 'bout faced and marched back to camp playing Yankee Doodle Quickstep. After "Monday the 9th" I will try to tell you of the proceedings.

This forenoon our Reg. went out for a grand target shoot but their targets being placed too far off not many of them were hit. Co. G succeeded in hitting theirs once. I do not want to have you think that the 16th are poor marksmen by the result of this shooting. The trouble was that the targets were placed beyond the range of our "Enfields" so you see that it was not the fault of the boys. But I am afraid that I am giving you too big a dose for once so I will bid you good night. With much love will I ever remain.

Your Aff Brother
Lyman B. Wilcox

Give my love to all.

L.

November 11, 1863
Camp of 16th Conn. Vols., Portsmouth, Va.

My very dear Robbie,

I believe that I promised to tell you about that execution that I was to attend. Last Friday was the day appointed for it. But for some cause or other it was postponed until Monday. Well Monday morning *[November 9]* we were up and had all of our camp duty done long before it was time for us to form. At 15 min before 8 our first call was sounded and at 8 the Regimental line was formed and immediately after we took the route for Fort Reno where the execution was to come off. The morning was very cold & chilly and for the first time this season our Reg. appeared with overcoats. At 9:30 we arrived on the ground and soon after the Guard with the prisoners came on to the ground. First came the Brigade Band playing a dirge, then a guard, next the two coffins bourne on two stretchers and then the Hacks containing the criminals and the Catholic Priests attending them. After them came another Guard which closed the procession. Immediately on arriving on the ground they proceeded within the square formed on three sides by the 8th, 15th, & 16th Conn. regt's. In the center of the other side was placed the two coffins side by side and the prisoners were placed blindfolded each in front of his own coffin and kneeling with their faces towards the guards who were to shoot them. After having their sentences read to them and a prayer by the Priests the Guard was placed about 6 paces from them and at the word "Fire" the poor miserable wretches paid for their desertion. It was a pretty hard sight but I do not think that there was a man in the whole Brigade that was sorry for they richly deserved it.

For fear that you may not understand it I will send you a rude sketch of the ground. Walter Smith arrived here yesterday. Good bye, write soon.

Your Aff Brother
Lyman B. Wilcox

Please excuse bad writing, in great hurry, Adieu. I should liked to have given you a more detailed account of the affair for it was very interesting to me at least, but not for kids.

Yours,
Lyman

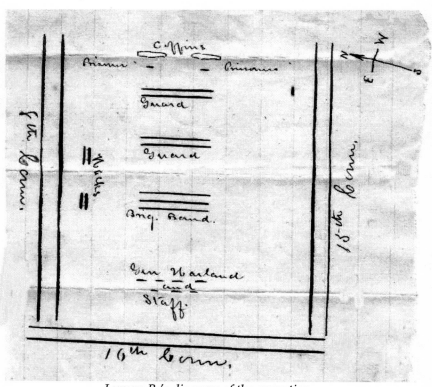

Lyman B.'s diagram of the execution

Chapter 6
Winter in Portsmouth, Virginia

The 16th Conn. enjoyed their continued stay in Portsmouth into early winter. Surgeon Nathan Mayer of the regiment spoke these words in his address at the Regiment 1867 reunion: "...the military standing of the regiment rose perceptively. There was not a cleaner, prompter, more loyal, reliable, and honest regiment in the service. No brighter arms, no quicker evolutions, no greater perfection in drill was to be found any where. The dress parade every evening gathered a crowd of lookers on. The guards, if detailed to other points, attracted attention, and the name of the Sixteenth was a good name in every man's mouth." (*B.F. Blakeslee, The History of the Sixteenth Connecticut Volunteers*)

November 29, 1863
Camp of 16th Conn. Vols., Portsmouth, Va.

My very dear Robbie,
 I hope that you will excuse me for not writing to you before but I have been so busy fixing up for winter quarters for the last week that I really have not found time. I have got bully quarters and I hope that I may stay here all winter to enjoy them.
 That Corp. Beanville that you wrote about is one of my tent mates. He is a first rate fellow. His real name is **WM. Johnson**.
 In one of your letters you spoke about having me get you some of these letters that we wear on our caps. I send you with this letter a copy of the "Old Dominion" with the letters inside of it. I tried to get you the "Musicians Bugle" but could only get the letters "G", "H", "C" "I".
 I hope that you will receive them safely. If you can Rob, I wish that you would send me that Book of Boats that is if you can

with out any trouble to yourself. But it is almost church time so I must bid you good bye. Love to all.

With much love I remain

Your Aff Brother

Lyman B. Wilcox

Johnson, *William; Private, Company E; Residence, Simsbury, Connecticut; Enlisted August 6, 1862; Mustered August 24, 1862; Wounded, Antietam, MD, September 17, 1862; Promoted to Full Corporal October 8, 1863; Captured at Plymouth, NC, April 20, 1864; Died December 25, 1864 at Andersonville, GA.*

December 15, 1863
Camp of 16th Conn. Vols., Portsmouth, Va.

My very dear Robbie,

I rec'd yours of the 9th this noon and having nothing else of importance to do just now I think that I will answer it. I am very glad to hear that you are agoing to school now and I hope that you will improve your time for this is probably the last opportunity that you will have for going to school. And Rob above all things take pains with your hand writing. If you only acquire a good style of hand writing it will be a fortune by itself to you. A good writer can get employment at almost any time. But so much for advice. I am probably in want of that article more than you are at present.

I am very glad to hear that you are all well and hope that you will continue so. Furloughs are played out now and for the present nobody can obtain one. So I think that I will not come home on a visit just yet.

I believe you asked me some time ago about our "Band". + I do not know whether I answered you or not, but for fear that I did not, I will give it to you in detail now. We have a first rate Brass Band in addition to the "Drum Corps" which is composed

90

of members of this Reg. It numbers 16 pieces now and the leader is our Former Chief Bugler. + taking it all together it is a first rate Regimental Band.

But adieu for the present. Excuse poor writing & the shortness of this letter. Give my best respects & love to Uncle Lester, Aunt Hattie + the children.

> With much love I remain
> You Aff Brother
> Lyman B. Wilcox

[Private Despatches]

Dear Rob. When I came away I left some pieces of ebony in my trunk I believe. What has been done with them and if they are in your possession could you get me a pair of Drumsticks turned out of them provided I send you a pattern & pay expenses. If you can you will greatly oblige.

> Lyme

January 1, 1864
Camp of 16th Conn. Vols., Portsmouth, Va.

My very dear Brother,

"Wish you a Happy New Year" and a very year I hope you may have of it too. We are not celebrating it any here except that almost all of the Reg. are drunk and last evening our "Band" played the old year out and the new year in. Some of the companies have got up celebrations on their own "hook" but I believe that it is only a partial success. Company "A" has a new years supper in our chapel to night and I think that you will see an account of it in next weeks "Hartford Post" for Prof. Beanville our "special correspondent" has been one of the invited guests.

By the way Rob, I am going to the Gettysville Theatre to night and enclosed I send you one of the "programmes". The musical director G. H Palmer is the leader of our Band. It is not a very big thing but old Johnson (or Prof. Beanville is the name that you will know him best by) has procured free tickets for the Drum Corps and we are all going "en masse".

Saturday morning – I did not have time to finish this letter last night and so I will finish it up now. We all went to the theatre and had a very good time last night except that our Drum Major was pretty drunk – ditto Johnson. The major was ejected for raining a disturbance and Johnson wound up by insulting an officer and getting put in the guard house where he remains now.

But no more at present. Enclosed you have the pattern for those sticks. Give my love & respects to all. With much love I remain

>Your Aff Brother
>Lyman B. Wilcox

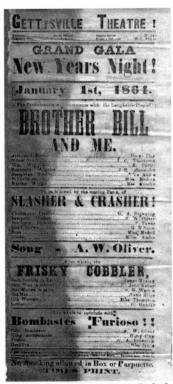

Gettysville Theatre program sent to Rob from Lyman B.

Winter in Portsmouth, Virginia

January 4, 1864
Camp of 16th Conn. Vols., Portsmouth, Va.

My very dear Brother,
    I rec'd yours of the 30th yesterday noon and am much obliged to you for your kind wishes. I am neither sick or in low spirits, but on the contrary am in the very best of spirits. I think that you must be enjoying yourself nicely at home by the way you passed your Christmas eve and by the number of presents that you received. You say that Leah ran away from her father. What was the cause of that. Please tell me all about the affair. The 31st we were mustered for two months pay – and if we get paid soon I may be able to send you something so that you can help Hattie as you say that you wish to so much. To day we rec'd 16 recruits for this Reg, and we shall soon be receiving more I think. Next month I understand that we are agoing to be allowed to re-enlist for 3 years from the 24th of March or the 1st of April and are to receive $792 bounty and 30 days furlough. That will make us five years service. But adieu for the present. I will look over my knapsack and see if I can find anything worth sending you for your museum.
    Give my love and best respects to all the folks at home and do your best at school for my sake. With much love I shall always remain
                Your Aff Brother
                Lyman B. Wilcox

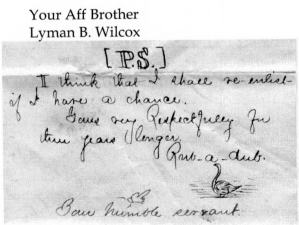

[P.S.]
I think that I shall re-enlist
if I have a chance.
      Yours very Respectfully for
three years (longer)
           Rub-a-dub.

Your humble servant.

Field Music: From Antietam to Andersonville

January 17, 1864
Camp of 16th Conn. Vols., Portsmouth, Va.

My dear Brother Robbie

Here is news at last. We are off for Newberne N.C. in the morning. We rec'd marching orders last night to be ready to go this morning but for some cause unknown to us "Privates" it was postponed until tomorrow morning.

It is rumored that we are going to reinforce Gen. Peck at Newberne and I think it is true though we cannot say for certain. But wherever we go you can direct your letters the same as before (Via Washington D.C.) and please write often. I should just like to have you look in upon us now and if you ever saw confusion you would see it here. When we rec'd marching orders last night we began to pack up our Knapsacks and the consequence is that our house looks like "a moving day in the city". My knapsack with all my extra clothing, blankets, overcoats etc. has assumed such gigantic proportions as to almost stagger me. But thank God I have only to carry it to Portsmouth, a distance of about 3 miles. From there we shall probably take an ocean transport and then Hurra! for Hatteras and an active campaign once more. And I am not sorry either for one. My next letter I think you will have from a state that you never rec'd one from before; that is the sacred soil more of old North Carolina. Well so goes the world. But Rob I wish that you was with us. If you enjoyed soldiering one tenth part as much as I do it would well repay you. But that is a forbidden subject so I will say no more about it for fear that I may possibly excite your warlike passions. Well I am rather glad that we are agoing to leave old Virginia for though it is the pleasantest place that that I have ever been in yet, still I wish to see some other part of this world. But as I am tired of writing and I suppose of course you must be tired of reading by this time I will close.

We do not get paid until the first of April now. Uncle Sam's "greenbacks" are running low and I expect he will have to strike off some more before he can pay us. Please ask Grandma to send me some Postage stamps and some "tin" if possible just a $

or so and it will make if all right in my next installment from my Uncle Samuel. These four cent stamps are the last that I have and these I had to borrow so you see that I cannot write any more until I get some more "<u>green</u> <u>backs</u>". Give love and best respects to all.

   With much love I remain
    Your Aff Brother
     Lyman B. Wilcox

P.S. I hope that you will excuse this bad writing for I am obliged to write on a table that is more than covered with dirty dishes.

   But with many good wishes
    I remain
     Lyman B.

Chapter 7
Plymouth, North Carolina

In early 1864, the 16th Conn. left Portsmouth, Virginia and traveled to Plymouth, North Carolina via river and sea. They were now deeply entrenched in the south. The Regiment engaged in a few small skirmishes over the course of the winter. They spent part of March in New Berne North Carolina, then traveled back to Plymouth in later March.

January 26, 1864
Camp of 16th Conn. Vols., Plymouth, N.C.

My very dear Robbie,
Once more I have an opportunity to write to you and before you will get this I think you may be glad to hear from me. In the first place I have since my last letter traveled over 500 miles and I am now at a place called Plymouth, a very small one horse town situated in the North-eastern part of North Carolina and forms the outpost of this department. We left Portsmouth on the morning of Thursday the 21st. Leaving our camp which was some 3 miles or more from the city at 8 O'clock we arrived in Portsmouth at about 10 and remained there until dark waiting for the transports. At 6 P.M. we went on board of the transport (a screw ocean steamer) "Fridette" and at 10 that night we weighed anchor and put out to sea. On this transport we were awfully crowded the most of us having to sleep on the deck the whole voyage. The next morning I was up with the sun but what a sight for a landsman. We were off Cape Henry but entirely out of sight of land, and Oh! My was not we pitching nicely but after awhile it was not quite so nice for I began to grow seasick and before long I was sick enough! But at noon I began to get my sea legs on and then I was all right for the rest of the voyage.

On Saturday morning we arrived at Beaufort, N.C. At 4 ½ O'clock P.M. we started on the cars for Newberne and got in there about 8 O'clock in the evening and immediately went on board of the transport "Pilot Bay". Leaving Newberne at midnight we arrived at Plymouth Monday morning and are now encamped near the city as it is called though it is no bigger than Berlin.

But I must close now, please excuse bad writing remembering that I am in a little shelter tent now and my writing facilities are none of the best.

I am very much obliged to you for those sticks and I wish that you would send them by mail, enclosed you will find a dollar to pay the postage with. If you do not seal the ends of the package the postage will not be very much.

> Your Aff Brother
> Lyman B. Wilcox

Direct same as before.

January 30th, 1864
Camp of 16th Conn. Vols., Plymouth, N.C.

Dearest Rob,

You cannot imagine what glorious old times I am having in this place. Our camp is close by the lordly old Roanoke river and I spend the most of my time on its bosom in a little dugout canoe that I have confiscated for that purpose. Her name is the "Calypso" and it is dug from the solid trunk of a Gum tree. Yesterday I went on an exploring expedition up one of the branches of the Roanoke but could discover nothing but swamps, and swamps there was on every side as far as the eye could reach. The trees in the swamp look as if they might be an hundred years old and are completely covered with a long grey moss which makes them look very old indeed and the water of the rivers here are just about the color of ale or any dark sweetened water. The peculiar color of the water is probably owing to their flowing through the swamps. There is one thing that is rather odd about these swamps (which cover the largest part of this state) which is that they are impenetrable by any human being, the under wood being so thick that it is impossible to go even a rod into them without cutting ones way with an axe and this is what the northern front of old North Carolina is mostly covered with, extending hundreds of miles.

And now let me describe little "Plymouth" to you. It is composed of about 50 houses, shops etc. I should think. There is a very few nice buildings, but the most of them are old and very ancient looking concerns compared with those in Northern villages. This town is situated close upon the bank of the Roanoke. How far from the mouth I cannot say as I was asleep when we came up on the boat and I have not been able to see a map since. But you can find it I think if you look at a map of N.C.

The most of the town is occupied by our troops who are quartered in the houses some of them and the remainder in tents on the "green". Our Brigade which is composed of the 15th & 16th Conn. are encamped about a half a mile from the town. There is 3 Regts from this place which are going home within a week or two as their time has expired and after then the garrison of this place will only be composed of this Brigade & 2 companies of New York Cavalry. So you see we are to have the place pretty much all to ourselves. It is rumored here now that Companies B. G. & K. are to go to Roanoke Island to do garrison duty and to be under command of our Senior Captain, **Capt Mix** of Co. B.

I hope that it will prove true for we can have a bully time there. But it will come somewhat harder on us Drummers as there is only two of us in the 3 companies that are to go. My friend "**Goodell**" of Co. B. and your humble servant of Co. G. but I guess that we can get through with it in some shape or other. But Robbie I guess that this letter is getting longer than you will care about reading, so I will shut her off. You need not be disappointed if you do not hear from me very often because sometimes a mail steamer does not leave hear once in a fortnight. But I will try and write you once in every two or three days so that you can get two or three at a time when you get any.

I have not received a letter from you for a long while but I expect to by the next steamer. Robbie I suppose it is needless to say that any thing in the shape of papers would be acceptable. We do not see a paper here once in a week and are in total ignorance of what is agoing on in the world around us. But enough for this letter so adieu.

> With much love I remain
> > Your Aff Brother
> > > Lyman B. Wilcox

Goodell, *Charles D.; Musician, Company H; Residence, Hartford, Connecticut; Enlisted August 12, 1862; Mustered August 24, 1862; Mustered out June 24, 1865.*

Mix, *Edward H.; Captain, Company B; Residence, Plymouth, Connecticut; Enlisted January 8, 1862; Drowned in Albemarle Sound, NC March 8, 1864.*

February 14th, 1864
Camp of 16th Conn. Vols., Plymouth, N.C.

My very dear Robbie,

To day is "St. Valentines" day but as I have no valentines to send I think I will write you a few lines even though you will not write to me.

To day is Sunday and I wonder how you are spending it at home. It is now about ½ past 3 O'clock in the afternoon and I think you must just about be coming out of church. But I will tell you how we are spending it here. We had our Reveille at sunrise as usual. At 7 the Breakfast call was sounded and we had our Breakfast which consisted of Bread & Coffee on the part of your humble servant. Some however could afford the luxury of having their Bread buttered and still others went so far as to have a cooked Breakfast (though these last were very few). At 8 we have a Surgeon's call when all of the sick report to the Surgeon's quarters for treatment. At ½ past 9 the call for Inspection was sounded and then our 4 Companies (those that are at this station) fell into line and we marched to the headquarters of the Regt, a distance of somewhat over a mile. Here we were joined by the remainder of the Regt., were formed in line of battle then wheeled into companies and each company inspected separately by the Colonel. After this was over (which lasted until near noon) we were marched back through the town to our quarters. Then our Dinner call was sounded and we had our Dinner which this noon consisted of Salt Junk (or Corned Beef I suppose is the proper name for it) and Potatoes. It was first rate what there was of it and enough of it such as it was that was all the trouble there was about it. We shall have a Dress Parade at 4:30 I suppose then after that the Supper call and then Supper which will be somewhat different from the Breakfast, that being Bread & Coffee and the Supper being Coffee & Bread.

Then Tattoo at 8 and Taps at 8:30 will close our "Sunday in the Army". It is somewhat different I think you will own then the way that you are spending it at home and of the two I much prefer our style though it would seem rather pleasant to walk into a Church instead of cleaning and polishing up for an inspection. But Robbie, probably before you receive this our time will be half up. Just think of it. The 24th of this month will find us just 18 months in the service of good old Uncle Samuel and just 18 months more will finish our job provided we do not re-enlist and that we live. Well that time will soon pass and then we shall have a chance to see old Connecticut once more. But I cannot say that I have any wish to see home just yet. For though it is as dear to me probably as to any one else, still I am not tired of a soldiers life yet, and not for worlds would I exchange my place for a situation at home.

But enough of that. Have you received any of my letters from this place. I have written several to you but have received no answer as yet. And it has been very near a month since I wrote the first one. What can it all mean. I do not for a minute doubt but that you have written to me but it is a mystery why I do not receive them. But I am living in hopes of hearing from you yet before my 3 years are up.

I say Robbie where is Uncle Edwin now. **Lieut. Miller** of our Company arrived here from recruiting at New Haven the other day and he says to me that he saw my Uncle at New haven, But he did not remember his name and that he enquired very particularly concerning me. Now do you suppose that it was Uncle Edwin or who was it. Lieut. Miller says that the gentleman was living at New Haven at the time he thought.

Robbie I positively must tear myself away so Adieu for the present.

My love to all & to yourself.

In hopes of some day stepping in and seeing you once more I remain

You very Aff. Brother
Lyman B. Wilcox

Miller, William; Corporal, Company E; Residence, Canton, Connecticut; Enlisted July 22, 1862; Mustered August 24, 1862; Promoted to Full Sergeant January 1, 1863; Promoted to Full 1st Sergeant February 5, 1863; Promoted to Full 2nd Lieutenant March 29, 1863; Promoted to Full 1st Lieutenant May 9, 1863; Discharged January 18, 1865.

March 15th, 1864
Camp of 16th Conn. Vols., Newberne, N.C.

My very dear Robbie,

I have not written to you for some time and the only reason was the want of writing papers and postage stamps. But this evening as I was lying in my bunk and thinking of days "lang syne" my thoughts very naturally reverted to you and how you would be disappointed if you did not hear from me so off I started for Co. G. and with some little trouble succeeded in rasing this sheet of paper and one postage stamp. Now you have the 'why and wherefore' that I have not written to you before.

But I suppose you would like to know how I came in New Berne so I will give you a short sketch of my adventures since my last letter to you. Thursday evening Mar 3rd I had no more idea of leaving our quarters at Plymouth than you probably have of leaving your quarters at N.B. *[New Britain]*. We beat our "Tattoo" at 8 o'clock and not ten minutes afterwards we rec'd our marching orders. At 8:30 we fell in with knapsacks packed with all of our worldly possessions and in just 15 minutes we were on board of the transport "Thomas Collyer" bound for New Berne.

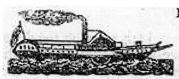

NOTICE.—The steamer THOS. COLLYER will not make her trip to Mount Vernon on Wednesday next, that day being a holyday, but will make her trips Thursday, January 2d, and Saturday, the 4th.

dec 31—2t   JOB CORSON.

The steamer "Thomas Collyer" continued to sail after the Civil War

That night we (the Drum Corps) slept on the hurricane deck, as did about half of the Regt. And I can assure you Robbie that if a fellow only thinks so he can sleep as well on the soft side of a plank yes, and better, than he can on a feather bed. In the morning when we awoke we were just off Roanoke Island and the fortifications could be seen very plainly from our perch on the upper deck. That day (Wednesday) was one of the most monotonous that I ever spent I think. For we were out of sight of land and there was nothing going on on board of our craft. But just about sunset we entered the "Neuse" river and the sight of land broke the monotony slightly.

Plymouth, North Carolina

The Neuse River in North Carolina

Darkness however soon put a stop to our land gazing, so reclining back on deck we passed a very pleasant evening telling stories and of the gay times that we should have when we once more could be at home. Ah! Robbie I wish that I could describe to you <u>that</u> scene but my pen is unequal to the task and I fear that it would only be a failure if I undertook it. But to realities. At about 10 o'clock we arrived in New Berne but for some cause we were not landed that night so I made my bed once more on the upper deck with my chum Charlie G. of Co. B. Very early in the morning we were astir and soon had our Knapsacks packed. We were then immediately marched on shore and marched then through the city of New Berne with Band playing and colors flying. After passing the city about a quarter of a mile we arrived at our present quarters which consist of first rate barracks built on the New Berne fair grounds. I have got a first rate bunk and I think that these are the best quarters that we have had since we came out. How long we shall stay here no one can tell, but the probabilities are that we shall move soon, but where to I cannot say.

Just a few rods from our barracks and within plain sight is the wreck of the gunboat "Underwriter" destroyed by the rebels when they attacked here not long ago *[February 1&2]*. I think you must have seen an account of it before this time and if you have seen the late illustrated papers you will have seen a picture of it. I have secured a piece of it for your museum which I will send you as soon as I can get a newspaper to put it in.

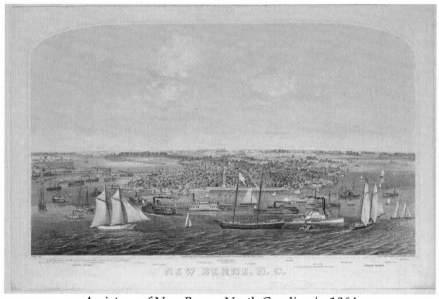

A picture of New Berne, North Carolina in 1864

I have just received a letter from Grandma and she speaks about your wishing to enlist. Now Robbie for my sake don't think of it any more. It is the very worst thing that you can do. Just make up your mind to bear a little longer and if you have chance try to learn a trade. It is the best thing that you can do if it is a trade that suits you. But if you don't have a chance, just wait until I get home and I will see what I can do for you. It will not be but 18 months longer at the furthest and I rather think Robbie that I can help you <u>some</u>. But enough for the present. Keep up good courage for you have not the worst place in the world. Give my love and respects to all.

     With much love I remain

     Your very Aff. Brother

       Lyman B. Wilcox

and if you have seen the late illustrated papers you will have seen a picture of it. I have secured a piece of it for your museum which I will send you as soon as I can get a newspaper to put it in.

I have just received a letter from Grandma and she speaks about your wishing to enlist. Now Robbie for my sake dont think of it any more it is the very worst thing that you can do. Just make up your mind to wait a little longer and if you have chance try to learn a trade, it is the best thing that you can do. if it is a trade that suits you. but if you dont have a chance. just wait until I get home and I will see what I can do for you. it will not be but 18 minutes longer at the furthest and I rather think Robbie that I can

Viewed sideways, you can see the ironclad ship Lyman B. drew on his last Civil War letter.

The above letter is the last known to have been sent by Lyman B. to his brother, Robbie, while on active duty during the Civil War. The 16th Conn., after returning from New Berne to the Union garrison at Plymouth, North Carolina, vigorously defended Plymouth and Fort Williams against a Confederate combined land and naval attack April 17-20, 1864 led by General Robert F. Hoke, C.S.A. Outnumbered more than 5 to 1, with no means of escape or opportunity for reinforcements, the Union garrison at Plymouth was surrendered on April 20, 1864 by Brigadier General Henry W. Wessells. These Union soldiers at Plymouth were known as the "Plymouth Pilgrims".

During the final hours of the Siege of Plymouth, a decision was made by Colonel Burnham to destroy the colors of the 16th Conn. Infantry. Col. Burnham took the colors, tore them into pieces, and gave pieces to the men around him. They concealed these pieces as they were captured and imprisoned.

The following letter from fellow soldier and Lyman B.'s cousin Samuel O. Fowler informs Robert Wilcox and other family members of Lyman B.'s capture.

From New Bern N.C. *[Samuel O. Fowler to Robert Wilcox]*
May 11, 1864

Dear Cousin,

I have written you one letter since my return to New Bern but do not know as you have received it. The papers inform us that the 16th Conn. regiment have been captured by the rebels with all forces under the command of the brave Gen. Wessels amounting in all to 1,800 men. Without doubt our dear Lyman is among the number. If you hear anything from him will you inform me of it. Last Friday about 5 P.M. the rebs came with a force of fifteen thousand men and three gunboats one being the ram Albermarle and the Cotton Plant and Bombshell.

Sketch of the C.S.S. Albemarle

Of the union forces there were gunboats engaged, the Cassius the Mattabeset and Philpiaton or some such name. We captured the Bombshell and the rest ran away and hid in the darkness of night. This is the same ram that went to Plymouth. The Bombshell was taken at the time of the capture of Plymouth and is the same boat we used to make raids into the enemys country – it carried four guns.

The 15th Conn are now doing Provost Guard duty in this city have been on this duty about two weeks. I am on guard at the mail warf today. The first guard duty I performed was at the market wharf. At this place everything is brought and as soon as the boats arrive each one has to report everything he has to the provost marshals before any sales can be made. Each guard on the wharf and at the office has a silver badge engraved the words "Provost Guard" this is worn on our coats to show who we are. We counted perhaps from 4 to 5 hundred dozen of eggs on that day. There were also came to market about 2 hundred bushels of oysters and a large quantity of fresh fish and also of salt ones. The oysters we eat all we wish to. One of the captains of the boats made two of us a present of 2 dozzen of eggs they sell at 25 cts per dozen. The prices are all fixed by the Provost marshal. Fresh fish 8 cts per pound. Oysters large one dollar & small 50 cts per bush. Presents of fish were also given to the guard. There were two boats came up the river and fired into by the rebs and told to go on shore. Some 12 shots were whizzing around and one struck the mast and the men saved the bullet. These were all darkies on board. They put on all sail and came as fast for New Bern as they could, arriving about 3 o'clock P.M. The sails of both boats were torn a number of places with bullets. News came to us last night of the spoiling of Gen. Lee's entire army – but it is too good to be true I fear. When that is done we may hope at peace again within our land when we can return to our homes – when we can talk over old time – so may the times speedydilly arrive. Robbie please write soon and often. Yours with aff esteem

Samuel O. Fowler

Chapter 8
Andersonville

In November, 1863, Confederate Captain W. Sidney Winder was sent to the village of Andersonville in Sumter County, Georgia, to assess the potential of building a prison for captured Union soldiers. The Confederate government had decided to relocate thousands of Union prisoners in and around the Richmond area to a place with more security and a more abundant food supply.

Andersonville, officially known as Camp Sumter, was a prison for captured enlisted Union soldiers. Opened in February, 1864, it was designed to hold 10,000 inmates within its 16 ½ acres. By August, 1864, the population had swelled to over 32,000, three times the original estimation. Even with the expansion of the prison to 26 ½ acres in June, 1864, Andersonville was atrociously overcrowded. The Confederate government could not provide adequate food, clothing, or medical care to Union captives. Available shelter was limited, consisting of shelters made of scrap wood, tent fragments, or holes dug in the ground. Many inmates had no shelter of any kind. No clothing was provided, with many prisoners being left with rags or no clothing at all. The diet was sparse.

These terrible circumstances created much suffering and a high mortality rate. During Andersonville's 14 month existence, almost 30% of the 45,000 prisoners confined to the camp died. Diseases such as dysentery, gangrene, diarrhea, and scurvy took many of these unfortunate.

These were the terrible conditions to which Lyman B. Wilcox was subjected after his regiment's capture in Plymouth, North Carolina. While many of the commissioned officers were sent to prison camps elsewhere, the enlisted men were sent to Andersonville. At the time Lyman B. and his fellow soldiers arrived, Andersonville's population was rapidly growing, but had not yet reached its height. Many soldiers of Lyman B.'s 16th

Connecticut Regiment continued to hide pieces of their colors in silent rebellion and pride. Whether Lyman was one of them, we do not know.

Andersonville Prison tents, August 17, 1864

We unfortunately have no letters from Lyman B. himself while he was at Andersonville. His close friend Charles Brandegee, however, was also imprisoned there and managed to send some letters home. In one of these letters, he indicated that Lyman B. was with him and that they "craved an exchange"[16] of prisoners.

Another Berlin native in Lyman B.'s Co. G, Jacob Bauer, wrote about his experience as a POW at Andersonville, and his experiences were probably similar, if not identical, to those of Lyman B. He wrote that, after capture, they were marched to

16 Livingstone, p. 131

Tarboro, North Carolina, and allowed to wash in the stream there. The prisoners were able to keep their valuables, but captors took canteens, blankets, and shoes for themselves. The captives were then loaded into cattle cars and packed in so tightly that they had to stand and could not move. The cars and tracks were in terrible shape, making the ride all the more difficult. Once at Andersonville, Jacob wrote that rations consisted of corn meal, which included the ground cob, and a small piece of bacon, often with maggots.

Other Berlin natives imprisoned at Andersonville included:

- **Andrew Bacon**. 14th Conn. Regiment, Co. F. Captured at Ely's Ford, VA. Transferred from Andersonville to a prison camp in Florence, SC, where he died on Jan. 25, 1865. His family helped carve the Civil War monument erected in 1871 in East Berlin.

- **William Barnum**. 16th Conn. Regiment, Co. G. Captured at Plymouth, NC and sent to Andersonville. Transferred to the prison camp at Florence, SC, where he died Jan. 15, 1865.

- **Reuben Barton**. 16th Conn. Regiment, Co. G. Captured at Plymouth, NC on Apr. 20, 1864 and sent to Andersonville. Paroled from the prison, but later died on Dec. 15, 1864.

- **Jacob Bauer**. 16th Conn. Regiment, Co. G. Captured at Plymouth, NC on Apr. 20, 1864. Sent to Andersonville and survived. Mustered out June 24, 1865.

- **Hiram Belden**. 16th Conn. Regiment, Co. G. Captured at Plymouth, NC on Apr. 20, 1864 and sent to Andersonville.

- **Orlando Belden**. Probably a relative of Hiram. 16th Conn. Regiment, Co. G. Captured at Plymouth, NC Apr. 20, 1864. Died on Feb. 28, 1865 after being paroled from Andersonville.

- **Charles Clifford**. 7th Conn. Regiment, Co. F. Captured at Bermuda Hundred, VA on Jun. 2, 1864 and sent to Andersonville. He survived the camp.

- **Burrage Deming**. 16th Conn. Regiment, Co. G. Captured at Plymouth, NC Apr. 20, 1864. Died of disease (diarrhea) at Andersonville on Nov. 13, 1864. He left behind a wife and young daughter.
- **David Ellsworth**. 18th Conn. Regiment, Co. C. Captured at Piedmont, VA Jun. 5, 1864 and sent to Andersonville. He survived and was discharged Jun. 5, 1865.
- **Nathan Gladwin**. 16th Conn. Regiment, Co. G. Captured at Plymouth, NC Apr. 20, 1864 and sent to Andersonville. Transferred to the prison camp at Florence, SC. Died in Florence on Oct. 12, 1864.
- **Charles Johnson**. 20th Conn. Regiment, Co. E. Captured at Plymouth, NC Apr. 20, 1864 and sent to Andersonville. He survived the camp and lived to at least 1907.
- **John Lawrence**. 16th Conn. Regiment, Co. E. Captured at Plymouth, NC and sent to Andersonville. He survived the camp.
- **Moses McCrum**. 16th Conn. Regiment, Co. G. Captured at Plymouth, NC on Apr. 20, 1864 and sent to Andersonville. Transferred to Charleston, SC, where he died on Oct. 2, 1864. An Irish immigrant, he left behind a wife and two children.
- **Edward Moore**. 16th Conn. Regiment, Co. G. Captured at Plymouth, NC Apr. 20, 1864 and sent to Andersonville. He survived the camp and was discharged on May 30, 1865.
- **Charles Richardson**. 16th Conn. Regiment, Co. G. Captured at Plymouth, NC on Apr. 20, 1864. Died of scorbutus (scurvy) as a prisoner at Andersonville Sep. 8, 1864.
- **Richard Ringwood**. 14th Conn. Regiment, Co. A. He died as a prisoner in Andersonville Aug. 25, 1864. An Irish immigrant, he left behind his wife Catherine.
- **Nelson Ritchie** 16th Conn. Regiment, Co. G. Captured at Plymouth, NC Apr. 20, 1864 and sent to Andersonville. He survived the camp and was mustered out Jun. 24, 1865.

- **Henry Savage.** 16th Conn. Regiment, Co. G. Captured at Plymouth, NC Apr. 20, 1864 and sent to Andersonville. He survived the camp and was mustered out Jun. 24, 1865.
- **Walter Smith.** 16th Conn. Regiment, Co. G. Captured at Plymouth, NC Apr. 20, 1864 and sent to Andersonville. He survived and was discharged May 27, 1865.
- **Henry and William Tibbals.** Henry Tibbals and his son, William, of East Berlin, CT, both belonged to the 16th Conn. Regiment, Co. G. Both father and son were captured at Plymouth, NC Apr. 20, 1864. Sadly, both father and son also died of disease (diarrhea) at Andersonville. Henry, the father, died on Jul. 31, 1864, and William died less than two weeks later on Aug. 12, 1864.

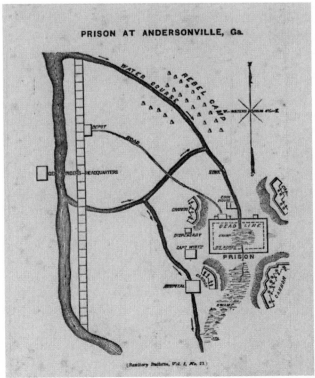

Map of Andersonville Prison, Georgia

Field Music: From Antietam to Andersonville

Samuel Fowler, who was not captured, wrote another letter to Robert Wilcox, indicating that Lyman B. was at Andersonville. Sadly, he was mistaken that it was "a very healthy place."

From New Bern N.C. [to Robert Wilcox]
May 18, 1864

Dear Cousin,
From all accounts the 16th regiment are now at Americus Georgia a very healthy place and if they do not starve them we think they will get along very well. We do think by all accounts Robbie that the rebels are now getting a terrible thrashing and beaten at all points what can they do but having for their end utter defeat their course now is hope less they are by all accounts coming into our lines by the thousands. One regiment is reported coming into the fortress yesterday. They are without rations and the poor fellows cannot live without something to eat – they tried to capture our supply train but failed in this also.
May we not hope that this terrible war will soon close but before that time arrives we expect Lyman and Henry Savage all of our friends will be set at liberty for our armies are now moving very swiftly and we expect our army soon to be at the rebs prisons to 'set all the captives free'. I am on guard in the city today but do not go on my post till night. This place is now in its beauty, the trees are dressed in their summer robes of green, fine old elms most of them are. The gardens can boast of fine lettuce and radishes and soon peas will be in abundance wherever planted. Last Sunday I attended church all day – after those services went a sabbath school in the lecture room near church. There were about 50 attended the school and there will be some esertions made to make the number one hundred and fifty schools are now in progress to teach all of the children in the place both white and black. There is no doubt but yankee influence will make the South what it never was in point of learning, and also of the arts and the arts and sciences – other

114

improvements will follow ??? as the country devellopes is resources.

I have just come to the post office to look at the bulletin for the news but there are none posted today. Please write to me soon and often. Remember me to all enquiring friends. Yours with aff esteem R.M.Wilcox

Samuel O. Fowler

Samuel was also overly optimistic about liberation, and the Andersonville captives were not freed by Union forces until May, 1865, a year after Samuel's letter. Many prisoners were paroled earlier, however, or sent to other prisons, such as at Florence, South Carolina. Catherine North, a late Victorian historian of Berlin, Connecticut, wrote in her "History of Berlin, Connecticut" that Lyman B. was also imprisoned at Florence[17], but evidence has not been found to support or refute the claim. As North was a relative of Lyman's, however, her account may well be reliable.

Whether at Andersonville or Florence, Lyman B. was paroled on December 10, 1864. Fellow Co. G soldier Jacob Bauer wrote that after release, "All of us who were not deathly sick were stripped and washed and our rags thrown overboard, lice & all. Everyone received a 30 day furlough home." [18] Lyman B. probably experienced the same treatment, after which he went home to recuperate.

Andersonville prison continued in use until the war ended in April, 1865. At this time, the prison's commandant, Captain Henry Wirz, was arrested and charged with war crimes including conspiracy and murder. The anger and outrage throughout the North over the conditions at Andersonville were somewhat appeased with the guilty verdict of Captain Wirz. He was hanged in Washington, DC, on November 10, 1865, the only person executed for war crimes during the Civil War.

---

17 North, p. 240
18 Bauer, Jacob. Personal experiences of the war of the rebellion. Kensington, Conn; January, 1915

Field Music: From Antietam to Andersonville

In summer, 1865, Clara Barton and a contingent of laborers and soldiers came to Andersonville to identify and mark the graves of the Union dead. Thanks to the records kept by a prisoner, Dorence Atwater, the majority of graves of those interred there could be identified and their families notified. Today, this cemetery is a monument to those soldiers.

In 1907, a beautiful statue, designed by Bela Lyon Pratt, was erected by the State of Connecticut at Andersonville to commemorate Connecticut soldiers once imprisoned there. Colonel Frank W. Cheney, a former member of the 16th Conn. Regiment also had a bronze replica made of the statue at his own expense, which he then donated to the State of Connecticut. This "Andersonville Boy" statue was erected on the Capitol grounds in Hartford, Connecticut. Both statues still stand to this day. Their dedication reads: *In memory of the men of Connecticut who suffered in Southern military prisons, 1861-1865."*

"Andersonville Boy" statue at the Connecticut State Capitol, Hartford

116

Chapter 9
After the War

Lyman B. Wilcox returned home after his parole in December, 1864. He may have come to Berlin to his grandmother's, or to one of his aunts' homes. Another prisoner, Walter Smith, stayed for a time with Dr. Brandegee, just up the road from Lyman B.'s grandmother. It is likely after his ordeal at Andersonville that Lyman was lice-ridden, emaciated, and weakened by illness and starvation. His friend Charles Brandegee would later write in his affidavit for Adeline Wilcox's 1881 widow's pension application that Lyman B. returned from imprisonment "a broken down man in mind and body."

Lyman B. had suffered countless bouts of dysentery and been exposed to an untold number of infections. The term 'post-traumatic stress disorder' would not exist for over one hundred years, yet after experiencing the horrors of war at its worst it would be a miracle if he didn't suffer from it. This would have manifested in a number of symptoms, such as anxiety, irritability, insomnia, nightmares, flashbacks, and would have been known at that time as 'Soldier's Heart'. In later times it would be called shell shock or combat fatigue.

In 1866, Lyman B. was living in Hartford, boarding on Center Street, and working as a bookkeeper.[19] He was able to recuperate enough to marry Adeline Sperry some time between 1865 and 1868. We do not know how or where they met or where she came from. There was a Sperry family in town, but the censuses of 1850 and 1860 have no mention of her. There were a number of Sperrys listed in the 1866 Hartford directory, but no mention of an Adeline. There was an Adeline Sperry of the approximate age living with a family in Manchester, Connecticut in 1860, but it is unclear if there is a connection.

---

[19] 1866 Hartford City Directory@Ancestry.com

Lyman B. and Adeline had a daughter, Ethel Adeline, born March 9, 1869, and a son, Lyman Harry, born December 10, 1871. In 1870 he and his family were living on Elm Street in New Britain, near the railroad tracks. He was a bookkeeper. His brother Robert was boarding with them. [20]

| *East Berlin Civil War Monument, ca. 1900* | *East Berlin Civil War Monument on Memorial Day, 2008* |

In 1871, the Washburn Chapter of the Grand Army of the Republic, a Union veterans' organization, erected a monument to the Berlin soldiers who had fallen during the Civil War. It is made of brownstone and similar in style to the Kensington monument. It is located in East Berlin at the junction of Main and Berlin Streets, across from Wilcox Cemetery. It is quite possible that Lyman B. attended the dedication, as he was a member of the G.A.R.

---

[20] New Britain City Directory, 1870-71

After the War

In 1873, Lyman B. was working for Taylor Manufacturing Co., makers of brass and hardware. Apparently he was having money problems, and had been out of work. The tone of these two letters to Rob shows Lyman to be dejected and depressed, a nearly broken man:

New Britain, Conn. Nov. 28th, 1873
My dear Rob,

Your letter of the 23rd inst. was rec'd a day or two since, and the contents done me good as usual. Am glad to hear that you got bravely over your cold. I thought you would not suffer from it long after you got in Boston. Am pleased to know that you have had such good success with new customers, but please Rob leave a few for me, out of pity at least. I am happy that you are preparing the way for me. It is a bully good thing to have an "advance courier" in this way, though if I had anything to say about it I should not go in for letting the "courier" take all the orders. Please excuse me for not writing you at Bangor. I did not notice until present reading of your letter that you gave me your address at that place. I mail you city papers by this mail. Did not receive them in time to send as I wrote you last. By the way, though, I find I did write you one letter at Bangor. I might have written you another if I had noticed the directions in your last letter in time. You will notice my Adr. in the Record. I have not received any benefit from it yet though. Think I shall make it more conspicuous in the next issue, so that it will attract more attention. I am at work at Taylors at present and have all I can do for some days at least. I do not know what I should do if it was not for that. It has nearly kept me in provisions so far. Taylor is feeling very blue indeed and is afraid to push his "bis" as I think he ought to at this time of year. He has called in Pierpont but has sent out Coggeshall on a trip up the Hudson. Taylor says he does not expect he will pay expenses and that is where I think he is foolish, when business is brightening up so much all over the country, as it appears to be at present.

How did you spend "Thanksmass". We had a very good time and quite unexpectedly too. Wednesday morning we rec'd a present from Grandma of two nice fat chickens for a "chickey pie" (as Harry calls it). We were obliged to accept them, as Grandma would not listen to any refusal at all. Then Thursday morning as we were getting ready to celebrate by ourselves, Aunt Mary sends over and insists upon us all coming over and eating dinner with them. Of course we could not refuse, so we went and had a very pleasant time indeed. Aunt Hattie, Uncle L. and the children came up in the evening and we had a good time generally, though the wish was expressed by everybody – "How I wish Rob was here" and "It does not seem like Thanksgiving without Rob here".

Thursday Dec. 4th – *Since writing the foregoing I have been so busy at Taylors that I have not found time to finish. I do not see why the deuce I have not heard from you before this. Is business so driving with you? I suppose you rec'd my letter at Bangor asking for small loan. If you do not find it convenient I trust you will let me know as soon as possible that I may try to make other arrangements. I find it very hard to collect from Taylor even what little he owes me.*

I should like to make that trip with you from Boston very much and I know it would be of great benefit to me, but I do not dare think of it on a/c of the expense it would be to you. By the way Rob, did you leave your last years overcoat out in Chicago with your other things. I wish I had the loan of it, for though I have plenty of coats they are not any of them fit to be seen in, outside of New Britain. As you are going west so soon though, I suppose you would not wish to send for it, and besides the expense in getting it here would be pretty heavy. I tell you Rob, I have been feeling very blue indeed to-day and I actually hope I may never live to be out of work again as I have this time. I have heard the saying "It is better to be out of the world than out of fashion" and I can say from the bottom of my heart – It is better to be out of the world than to be out of work. That is not a very courageous expression, I know. And I do not feel courageous the slightest in the world. I am completely cowed I think. I have always felt hitherto that I was bound to succeed and come out all right in the end, but I begin to doubt it now. When I look back and find that I am not one bit better off than I was three years ago – that my labor for that time has been only a struggle to keep alive – well, where is the use in trying – I am beaten and will own it up. However such thoughts are best kept to oneself I suppose. I have made many mistakes in this world and I suppose it but right that I should suffer the consequences.

But I must close. Am sorry that I have not any good news to communicate to you, but such is life with me. Uncle Lester moved into the Franklin St. house last week and are quite near to us now. Hope to hear from you soon. Ethie has been quite sick but is getting better now. The rest of us are all well as usual. With much love I am
    Your Affectionate Brother,
    Lyman B. Wilcox

Robert, on the other hand, became quite successful. He spent time travelling and working in sales for the Taylor Co. and others over the next few years. He also worked for a time in Hartford as a printer's apprentice and became a compositor at the Meriden Recorder. Their sister Hattie married Leander Bunce of Kensington, a well-respected farmer, and became a charter member of the local chapter of the Daughters of the American Revolution. She and her husband adopted a daughter, Kate. They are buried in Maple Cemetery, Berlin.

We have no further word about Lyman B. after the above letter until his death on May 29, 1875 at the age of 30. A notice in the New Britain Record of June 4, 1875 informed of his death:

"In Greenville, S.C., Lyman B. Wilcox, formerly of Hartford, Conn., aged 30 years & 4 months. Prayer at the residence of Mrs. Ruth Bulkley, 37 Franklin St., N.B. Friday June 4 at 11/2 o'clock. Funeral services in the Cong. Church, Berlin at 3 o'clock. Relatives and friends are invited to attend." [21]

---

[21] New Britain Record, 6/4/1875

Lyman B. was buried in Maple Cemetery in Berlin, Connecticut. His obelisk monument bears a striking resemblance to the two Civil War monuments in town. His epitaph reads:

> *In the War of the Rebellion*
> *A Faithful Soldier.*
> *Lay Him in the Sunshine nor Sorrow*
> *That a Christian Hath Departed.*

Closeup of Lyman B. Wilcox's grave, showing his epitaph.

At the time of his death, Lyman B.'s daughter Ethel was 6, and his son Lyman Harry only 3 ½. The tradition of early death had continued through three generations. It is easy to raise questions as to the cause of his death. Was it related to his war service and imprisonment? Did he inherit his father's asthma? Was it self-inflicted, an accident, or due to foul play? What was he doing in South Carolina? Was his family there with him? The records are silent.

Left: Lyman B. Wilcox's obelisk-shaped grave, with his individual grave marker in front accompanied by an American flag. Lyman B. shares the obelisk with his Uncle Frank and Aunt Mary Chambers and their family in Maple Cemetery, Berlin, Connecticut.

Above: Lyman B.'s individual grave marker marking where his body was laid to rest.

After Lyman B.'s death, Adeline, Ethel and Lyman H. initially lived in New Britain. Ethel sent the following letter to Robert in 1877:

DEAR uncle ROB

I have BRUSHED my
teeth every DAy. I am
in the secoND Reader.
Ruth Has passed in
IDiTHS RooM

yours with love
Ethel.

The "Ruth" mentioned was probably Lyman B.'s grandmother Ruth Savage Bulkley, who died on November 5, 1877. On the back of the letter, Ethel drew this picture:

Adeline and her children made a home with Lyman B.'s brother, Robert Wilcox in the late 1870s. Robert began a correspondence with famed poet and author Ella Wheeler which culminated in their marriage in 1884. During this time he moved from New Britain to Meriden and began working for the Britannia Silver Co. Eventually, Robert and Ella Wilcox moved to Short Beach in Branford, Connecticut, where their collection of homes on the Long Island Sound became known as Bungalow Court. Robert still remembered his hometown, however. He donated a prize, the Bulkley Cup, which was awarded annually at the Berlin Fair.

Robert also kept the letters that Lyman B. had written him, as well as many others. Perhaps Robert remembered, in all his success, how his brother strove to protect him. He died in Short Beach, Branford in 1916. His wife, Ella Wheeler Wilcox, died of cancer not long after in 1919. Their ashes are interred on their estate in Short Beach.

*Photos of Robert Wilcox (left)
and Ella Wheeler Wilcox (right)*

Adeline Wilcox applied for a widow's pension in 1881, but there is no evidence that her application was granted. When Adeline's children reached adulthood, she moved with them to Antioch, Oregon, where Lyman H. worked as a farmer on his own fruit farm. Around 1909, Ethel married Fred H. Hauptman, the son of German and French immigrants. They divorced soon after, and Ethel seems to have changed her name back to 'Wilcox' between the 1920s and 30s. Lyman H. never married.

After their mother Adeline died in 1923, Lyman H. and Ethel moved to California. According to the 1930 and 1940 censuses, Lyman H. and his sister Ethel then lived together on Commercial Place, a street of small stucco houses in Los Angeles, California. Ethel worked as an interior decorator and Lyman H. held various jobs, including a refrigerator salesman and decorator in the plastic relief industry. Ethel lived until 1955 and died in California. Lyman Harry Wilcox broke the trend of the Lymans; he died in Los Angeles in 1961, in his 90th year.

After the War

As for the legacy of the 16th Connecticut Volunteer Infantry, they became known as the 'Hard Luck' Regiment. Numbers tell the story:

Overall statistics from August, 1862 until April, 1865:
- *Original Muster:* 1007
- *Recruits during the war:* 80
- *Total 16th Conn.:* 1087

Casualties:
- *Deaths:*
  - o *Killed in Action:* 47
  - o *Died of Wounds:* 45
  - o *Died of Disease:* 73
  - o *Died in Prison:* 178
  - o *Lost at Sea, Drowning:* 10
  - o *Total Deaths:* 353
- *Captured:*
  - o *At Antietam* 12
  - o *At Plymouth* 435
  - o *Total Captured:* 447
- *Wounded & Missing:*
  - o *Wounded:* 212
  - o *Missing:* 56
  - o *Total:* 268

Discharged prior to Jun 1865: 386

The Regiment arrived in Hartford, Connecticut on June 29, 1865 at 8 a.m. at the Asylum Street depot. Sadly, only 131 of the regiment returned on this day. It is not known if Lyman B. traveled to Hartford to witness the event.

From the Hartford Courant, June 30, 1865:
"Everybody supposed that this gallant regiment would arrive here on the 9:45 regular morning accommodation train from New Haven, but the "boys" being accustomed to making surprises secured special transportation and were in the Asylum

> *Street depot by 8 o'clock. Here they were received by the Governor's Guard, the City Guard, and Colt's band, and escorted up High to North Main Street, down Main to State. On the march, though few in numbers, (but one hundred and thirty enlisted men returning) their tidy and soldierly appearance was the subject of general comment. Being a Hartford regiment there was an unusual interest manifested to see them, and signs of welcome were apparent on every hand. Arriving in front of the United States Hotel, they were drawn up in line, and Governor Buckingham made a brief speech congratulating them on their safe return and extending them cordial greetings on behalf of the State."*

Later, in 1879, in preparation for Battle Flag Day at the Connecticut State Capitol, a committee of 16th Conn. veterans wanted to reassemble the colors. They sent letters to all members asking for the pieces of the colors they had hidden before their capture in Plymouth, North Carolina on April 20, 1864. Not all were recovered, but they received enough to make the central device on a new flag. Tiffany & Company made the flag for $325.00.

The inscription embroidered on the bottom of the flag is as follows:

> *"The device on this flag is composed entirely of fragments of the old colors of the 16th Reg't Conn. Vols. They were torn into shreds by the officers and men, and concealed upon their persons in order to save them from the enemy at the Battle of Plymouth, N.C., April 20, 1864, where together with the whole Union force at that post, the regiment after a three days fight against overwhelming numbers was compelled to surrender. Many of the men bearing these relics were taken to Southern prisons, where under untold privations, they still sacredly watched over and kept their trusts, subsequently returning them to their native State."*

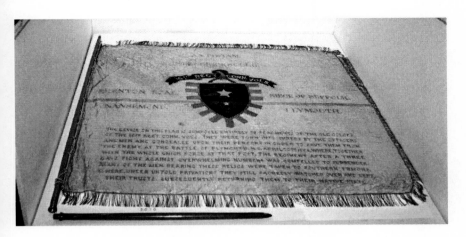

This pride of the 16th Conn. was brought back to life in this Commemorative Flag, which is displayed proudly at the State of Connecticut Capitol in Hartford.

Through the flags and statues at the Connecticut Capitol, the monuments at Antietam and Andersonville, the local memorials, and the many correspondence, journals and testaments from soldiers like Lyman B. Wilcox, the memory of the trials and triumphs of the 16th Connecticut Volunteer Infantry lives on. From Officer to Drummer Boy, we give them our thanks.

Photo and Illustration Credits

Front   Drummers packed for Marching Orders
Cover   Drawn by Lyman B. Wilcox, ca. 1862
         Courtesy of Berlin Historical Society

Title   Lyman B. Wilcox
Page   Photo by Camp Photographers, Hartford, CT, ca. 1873
         Courtesy of Berlin Historical Society

7   Kensington Civil War Monument
         Postcard, ca. 1910
         Courtesy of Berlin Historical Society

17   Smith's 1855 Map of Hartford County
         Photo by Nancy Moran, ca. 2012
         Courtesy of Berlin Historical Society

18   Smith's 1855 Map of Hartford County
         Photo by Nancy Moran, ca. 2012
         Courtesy of Berlin Historical Society

20   Lyman B.'s first home on Toll Gate Road, Berlin, CT
         Photo by Sarah Caliandri, ca. 2012

22   Belcher Brook, Berlin, CT
         Photo by Lisa M. Jacobs, ca. 2010

24   Worthington Ridge, Berlin from the North
         Unknown, ca. 1836
         Courtesy of Nancy Moran

26   Lyman and Maria Wilcox's gravestones, Wilcox Cemetery,
         East Berlin, CT
         Photo by Lisa M. Jacobs, ca. 2012

Photo and Illustration Credits

29   Envelope
Drawn by Lyman B. Wilcox, ca. 1859
Courtesy of Berlin Historical Society

31   Grave of Josiah Wilcox, Wilcox Cemetery, East Berlin, CT
Photo by Lisa M. Jacobs, ca. 2007

32   Berlin Town Clerk Office enlistment records from 1862
Photo by Nancy Moran, ca. 2012

34   16th Conn. Regiment color flag at Connecticut State Capitol
Courtesy of Bill Caughman

37   Statue of Gen. Sedgwick on Connecticut Capitol Building
Photo by Lisa M. Jacobs, ca. 2012

40   Letter by Lyman B. Wilcox, ca. 1862
Courtesy of Berlin Historical Society

41   Monument to 16th Conn. Regiment at Antietam
Photo by Albert Muratori

43   President Lincoln talking to troops at Antietam, ca. 1862
Postcard
Courtesy of Nancy Moran

47   Drummers packed for Marching Orders
Drawn by Lyman B. Wilcox, ca. 1862
Courtesy of Berlin Historical Society

49   Grave of Henry Tibbals, Wilcox Cemetery, East Berlin, CT
Photo by Lisa M. Jacobs, ca. 2007

54   Letterhead showing Newport News, VA
Lithograph by E. Sacshe & Co., Baltimore; Published by C.
Bohn, Washington, DC, ca. 1861
Courtesy of Berlin Historical Society

55   Letterhead showing Peck's Headquarters at Suffolk, VA
Sketch by C. Worret; Published by C. Bohn, ca. 1863
Courtesy of Berlin Historical Society

58   Moses McCrum's grave, Wilcox Cemetery, East Berlin, CT
Photo by Lisa M. Jacobs, ca. 2007

64   Civil War drummers
Unknown, ca. 1861-1865
Courtesy of Steve Buckley

74   Samuel Woodruff's grave, Maple Cemetery, Berlin, CT
Photo by Lisa M. Jacobs, ca. 2012

76   Diagram of Lyman B. Wilcox's tent and camp
Drawn by Lyman B. Wilcox, ca. 1863
Courtesy of Berlin Historical Society

84   Civil War field musicians
Unknown, ca. 1861-1865
Courtesy of Steve Buckley

88   Diagram of an execution
Drawn by Lyman B. Wilcox, ca. 1863
Courtesy of Berlin Historical Society

92   Gettysville Theatre program for Jan. 1, 1864
Courtesy of Berlin Historical Society

93   Excerpt of Lyman B. Wilcox letter, ca. 1864
Courtesy of Berlin Historical Society

Photo and Illustration Credits

102   Newspaper notice re: steamer Thos. Collyer
Courtesy of Steve Buckley

103   Neuse River in North Carolina
Photo by Ken Thomas, ca. 2005

104   New Berne, North Carolina in 1864
Lithograph by Major & Knapp Engraving, ca. 1864
Courtesy of New York Public Library Digital Collection

105   Letter and drawing of ironclad ship
Drawn by Lyman B. Wilcox, ca. 1864
Courtesy of Berlin Historical Society

107   C.S.S. Albemarle
Drawing by R. G. Skerrett, ca. 1899
Courtesy of the Navy Art Collection, Washington, DC

110   Andersonville prison
Photo by Unknown, ca. 1864
Courtesy of Civil War Photograph Collection, Library of Congress

113   Map of Andersonville prison
Courtesy of Steve Buckley

116   "Andersonville Boy" statue, Capitol grounds, Hartford, CT
Photo by Lisa M. Jacobs, ca. 2012

118   (Left) East Berlin Civil War Monument, ca. 1900
Courtesy of Berlin Historical Society

118   (Right) East Berlin Civil War Monument
Photo by Lisa M. Jacobs, ca. 2008

122   Detail of Lyman B. Wilcox's gravestone
Photo by Lisa M. Jacobs, ca. 2012

Bibliography

Adams, Charles Collard. Middletown Upper Houses: a history of the north society of Middletown, CT from 1650 to 1800.New York: Grafton Press, 1908

Ancestry.com American Civil War Soldiers

Ancestry.com Andersonville Prisoners of War

Ancestry.com Family Trees

Ancestry.com New Britain City Directories

Ancestry.com U.S. Census Records

Ancestry.com U.S. Civil War Soldiers 1861-1865

Andrews, Alfred. New Britain genealogy and ecclesiastical history Chicago, IL: A. H. Andrews, 1867

Bauer, Jacob. Unpublished manuscript of reminiscences of the Civil War, at Berlin-Peck Memorial Library, 1916

Berlin, CT Land Records

Berlin, CT Probate Records

Berlin, CT Vital Records

Blakeslee, B. F. History of the Sixteenth Connecticut Volunteers. Hartford, CT: The Case, Lockwood & Brainard Co., 1875

http://www.boltoncthistory.org/charleslyman2

http://www.civilwararchive.com

http://www.civilwarintheeast.com

Heritagequest Online Revolutionary War Pension Applications

Historical Data Systems, comp.. *U.S. Civil War Soldier Records and Profiles* [database on-line]. Provo, UT, USA: Ancestry.com Operations Inc, 2009.

Livingstone, Charles B. Charlie's Civil War. Gettysburg, PA: Thomas Publications, 1997

Kensington Congregational Church 200th anniversary, Kensington, CT, unknown, 1912

Nash, Elizabeth Todd: Fifty Puritan Ancestors, 1628-1660. New Haven, CT: Tuttle, Morehouse & Taylor, 1902

National Archives and Records Administration. *Civil War Pension Index: General Index to Pension Files, 1861-1934* [database on-line]. Provo, UT, USA: Ancestry.com Operations Inc, 2000.

Field Music: From Antietam to Andersonville

New Britain City directories, 1870-71, 1871-72, 1872-73, 1876 at the
    Local History Room, New Britain Public Library
New Britain City directories, 1874-75 at CT State Library
New Britain Record microfilm at the CT State Library
North, Catharine. History of Berlin, Connecticut New Haven, CT:
    Tuttle, Morehouse & Taylor, 1916
Smith's Map of Hartford County, 1855 at the Berlin Historical
    Society Museum
Stub, Lorraine. Simeon North and the mill on Spruce Brook, in
    The Berlin Citizen, Jul. 26, 2012 and Aug. 2, 2012
http://www.unionvolunteersfifeanddrum.com
http://www.vermontcivilwar.org

About the Publisher

Berlin Historical Society
PO Box 8192
305 Main Street
Kensington, CT 06037
(860) 828-5114

Our museum dedicated to Berlin, Connecticut history is open Saturdays, 1:00 – 4:00 pm from April through December. We are also open for tours or research by appointment.

About the Authors

Sarah (Sallie) Caliandri grew up in an old farmhouse in Berlin, where her family has lived for over 100 years. Her mother, a teacher, told many stories, and Sallie delighted in hearing tales of the "old days" of the 1920s and 1930s when the civil war veterans would ride in the parades, their long beards flowing. Trips to the CT State Library and to cemeteries in search of family history contributed to her lifelong love of history and genealogy. She is a board member of the Berlin Historical Society. Sallie has written a number of articles for the Berlin Citizen and for the Historical Society, and is currently working on a history of Berlin. This is her first book. She has spoken on a variety of topics related to Berlin history.

On a personal note, she lives in Berlin with her husband Don, with her two sons not far away. She continues her mom's legacy by teaching family and Berlin History to her four grandchildren.

Lisa Marie Jacobs grew up in an old house, built in 1822 by Benjamin Wilcox (a great-great uncle of Lyman B. Wilcox) in East Berlin, CT. Raised by parents with a love of history, she now works with them selling antiques and also serves on the Board of the Berlin Historical Society. She also enjoys historical research, genealogy and photographing cemeteries and historic sites, both as art and for posterity. Similarly, Lisa has written avidly since childhood, including essays, poetry and fiction, and has a passion for wildlife and natural photography. This is her first non-fiction publication, though her poetry and photography have appeared elsewhere.

Nancy Moran developed her interest in local history after purchasing and lovingly restoring an old home in the historic district of Berlin, CT. She has been active in the Berlin Historical Society for many years, and is currently on the Board of Directors. She dabbles in writing historical sketches as well as short stories with family connections. This is her first venture in co-authoring and publishing a book. Nancy is also a student of the Civil War, especially Gettysburg, which she visits annually on the battle anniversary. She has stood in the Antietam cornfield where the 16th Conn. had its inaugural engagement. Nancy and her husband, Rick, enjoy time with their four sons and wives, family and friends. They continue to lovingly care for their old home, which is located a scant half mile from Lyman B. Wilcox's grandmother's home.